CROCHETING RUFFLED DOILIES

EDITED BY
Linda Macho

Dover Publications, Inc., New York

Stitch Conversion Chart

U.S. Name	Equivalent
Chain	Chain
Slip	Single crochet
Single crochet	Double crochet
Half-double or short-double crochet	Half-treble crochet
Double crochet	Treble crochet
Treble crochet	Double-treble crochet
Double-treble crochet	Treble-treble crochet
Treble-treble or long-treble crochet	Quadruple-treble crochet
Afghan stitch	Tricot crochet

Hook Conversion Chart

Aluminum

U.S. Size	B	C	D	E	F	G	H	I	J	K
British & Canadian Size	12	11	10	9	8	7	5	4	3	2
Metric Size	2½	3	—	3½	4	4½	5	5½	6	7

Steel

U.S. Size	00	0	1	2	3	4	5	6
British & Canadian Size	000	00	0	1	–	1½	2	2½

General Instructions

* (Asterisk) : This symbol indicates that the instructions immediately following are to be repeated the given number of times plus the original.

**Are used in same way for a second set of repeats within one set of directions.

Repeat instructions in parentheses as many times as specified. For example: "(Ch 5, sc in next sc) 5 times" means to work all that is in parentheses 5 times in total.

CROCHET ABBREVIATIONS

ch	Chain
st	Stitch
sl st	Slip st.
s c	Single Crochet
s d c	Short Double Crochet
d c	Double Crochet
tr c	Treble Crochet
d tr c	Double Treble Crochet
tr tr c	Triple Treble Crochet
o m	Open Mesh. Sometimes termed sp-Space
s m	Solid Mesh. Sometimes termed bl-Block
p	Picot
d p	Double Picot
beg. rnd	Beginning Round
incl	Inclusive
inc	Increase
dec	Decrease

Copyright © 1982 by Dover Publications, Inc.
All rights reserved under Pan American and International Copyright Conventions.

Published in Canada by General Publishing Company, Ltd., 30 Lesmill Road, Don Mills, Toronto, Ontario.
Published in the United Kingdom by Constable and Company, Ltd., 10 Orange Street, London WC2H 7EG.

This Dover edition, first published in 1982, is a new selection of patterns from *Star Gift Book, Knit/Crochet/Tat*, Book No. 31, published by The American Thread Company, Inc., New York, in 1944; *Doilies: A Collection of Fascinating New Designs*, Book No. 235, published by The Spool Cotton Company, New York, in 1947; *Ruffled Doilies and the Pansy Doily*, Star Book No. 59, published by The American Thread Company, Inc., in 1948; *Ruffled Doilies*, Book No. 253, published by The Spool Cotton Company in 1949; *Ruffled Doilies*, Star Doily Book No. 95, published by The American Thread Company, Inc., in 1952; *Doilies*, Star Doily Book No. 128, published by The American Thread Company in 1956; *Doilies*, Star Doily Book No. 131, published by The American Thread Company in 1956; *Doilies to Treasure*, Book No. 1600, published by the Lily Mills Company, n.d.; *The Famous Puritan Crochet Book*, Star Puritan Book No. 114, published by The American Thread Company, n.d.; *Doilies*, Star Book No. 172, published by The American Thread Company, n.d.

Manufactured in the United States of America
Dover Publications, Inc., 180 Varick Street, New York, N.Y. 10014

Library of Congress Cataloging in Publication Data
Main entry under title:

Crocheting ruffled doilies.

(Dover needlework series)
1. Crocheting. 2. Doilies. I. Macho, Linda, 1955- . II. Series.
TT825.C757 1982   746.9'6041   82-9497
ISBN 0-486-24400-8   AACR2

Introduction

Through the years, fashions in home decorating have run full cycle. Who can forget those days-gone-by when our parents and grandparents graced their tables, bureaus and buffets with frilly, ruffled doilies? Now, once again, ruffled doilies are in the limelight of popularity, beguiling crocheters with the romance of frothy, almost frivolous lace. For many crocheters, the most difficult aspect of crocheting ruffled doilies has been locating good patterns; this book now ends that search. Here is a new collection of 33 beautiful ruffled doily patterns originally published over thirty years ago in instruction brochures.

Although many of the threads listed with the patterns are still available, you may wish to substitute some of the newer threads now on the market. Check with your local needlework shop or department and buy thread that is compatible with the recommended hook size. Whatever type of thread you decide to use, be certain to buy a sufficient amount of the same dye lot to complete the project; it is often impossible to match shades later because of the variation in dye lots.

All of the stitches used in the projects in this book are explained on page 4; a list of crochet abbreviations and General Instructions appears on the page facing this one.

For perfect results, the number of stitches and rows should correspond with those indicated in the directions. Before starting your ruffled doily, make a small sample of the stitch, working with the suggested hook and desired thread. If your working tension is too tight or too loose, use a larger or finer crochet hook to obtain the correct gauge.

When you have completed your doily, it should be washed, starched and blocked. Use a good neutral soap or detergent and make suds in warm water. Wash by squeezing the suds through the doily, but do not rub. Rinse two or three times in clear water and squeeze out the excess water.

There are several ways to starch your doilies. Three methods are explained here; two are the tried-and-true, old-fashioned methods, and the third is a method using a new product manufactured specifically for starching doilies.

METHOD 1: Starch: Dissolve ¼ cup starch in ½ cup of cold water. Boil about 1¼ cups of water, remove from flame, then slowly stir the starch mixture into boiling water, stirring constantly. Place back on flame until the mixture thickens.

Directions: As soon as the starch is cool enough to handle, dip doily and squeeze starch through it thoroughly. Wring out extra starch. The doily should be wet with starch but there should be none in the spaces. Pin center of doily in position according to size and leave until thoroughly dry. If a steam iron is used, iron ruffle after it is dry. If a regular iron is used, dampen ruffle slightly before pressing. Pin folds of ruffle in position and leave until thoroughly dry.

METHOD 2: Starch: Dissolve ¼ cup starch in ½ cup of cold water. Boil slowly over a low flame; as it thickens, gradually stir in about 1¼ cups of cold water. Boil, stirring constantly, until starch clears. This makes a thick, pasty mixture.

Directions: Follow directions given in Method 1.

METHOD 3: Doily Dip™: *Doily Dip* is a concentrated water-based polymer to be used with cloth, lace, crochet or paper; it stiffens your favorite design or project quickly and easily. *Doily Dip* can be found in many needlework and craft shops or by writing to Hazel Pearson Handicrafts, 16125 E. Valley Blvd., City of Industry, CA 91744.

Directions: *Doily Dip* can be diluted two to one; for every two ounces of *Doily Dip*, add one ounce of water. Pour *Doily Dip* solution into a container large enough for the crocheted project and the liquid. Dip crochet into liquid and squeeze or press out excess solution. DO NOT WRING. Pin center of doily in position according to size and leave overnight until thoroughly dry. To speed drying, place project in a well-ventilated warm area. NOTE: Excess *Doily Dip* may cause white residue when dry; to remove, heat oven to 300°, turn oven off, and place project in warm oven for about 10 minutes. If a steam iron is used, iron ruffle after it is dry. If a regular iron is used, dampen ruffle slightly before pressing. Pin folds of ruffle in position and leave until thoroughly dry.

The crochet terminology and hooks listed in this book are those used in the United States. The charts opposite give the U.S. name of crochet stitches and their equivalents in other countries and the equivalents to U.S. crochet hook sizes. Crocheters should become familiar with the differences in both crochet terms and hook sizes before starting a project.

Simple Crochet Stitches

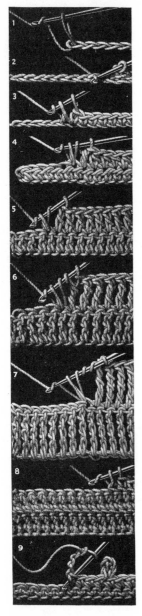

No. 1—Chain Stitch (CH) Form a loop on thread, insert hook on loop and pull thread through tightening threads. Thread over hook and pull through last chain made. Continue chains for length desired.

No. 2—Slip Stitch (SL ST) Make a chain the desired length. Skip one chain, * insert hook in next chain, thread over hook and pull through stitch and loop on hook. Repeat from *. This stitch is used in joining and whenever an invisible stitch is required.

No. 3—Single Crochet (S C) Chain for desired length, skip 1 ch, * insert hook in next ch, thread over hook and pull through ch. There are now 2 loops on hook, thread over hook and pull through both loops, repeat from * For succeeding rows of s c, ch 1, turn insert hook in top of next st taking up both threads and continue same as first row.

No. 4—Short Double Crochet (S D C) Ch for desired length thread over hook, insert hook in 3rd st from hook, draw thread through (3 loops on hook), thread over and draw through all three loops on hook. For succeeding rows, ch 2, turn.

No. 5—Double Crochet (D C) Ch for desired length, thread over hook, insert hook in 4th st from hook, draw thread through (3 loops on hook) thread over hook and pull through 2 loops thread over hook and pull through 2 loops. Succeeding rows, ch 3, turn and work next d c in 2nd d c of previous row. The ch 3 counts as 1 d c.

No. 6—Treble Crochet (TR C) Ch for desired length, thread over hook twice insert hook in 5th ch from hook draw thread through (4 loops on hook) thread over hook pull through 2 loops, thread over, pull through 2 loops, thread over, pull through 2 loops. For succeeding rows ch 4, turn and work next tr c in 2nd tr c of previous row. The ch 4 counts as 1 tr c.

No. 7—Double Treble Crochet (D TR C) Ch for desired length thread over hook 3 times insert in 6th ch from hook (5 loops on hook) and work off 2 loops at a time same as tr c. For succeeding rows ch 5 turn and work next d tr c in 2nd d tr c of previous row. The ch 5 counts as 1 d tr c.

No. 8—Rib Stitch. Work this same as single crochet but insert hook in back loop of stitch only. This is sometimes called the slipper stitch.

No. 9—Picot (P) There are two methods of working the picot. (A) Work a single crochet in the foundation, ch 3 or 4 sts depending on the length of picot desired, sl st in top of s c made. (B) Work an s c, ch 3 or 4 for picot and s c in same space. Work as many single crochets between picots as desired.

No. 10—Open or Filet Mesh (O M) When worked on a chain work the first d c in 8th ch from hook * ch 2, skip 2 sts, 1 d c in next st, repeat from *. Succeeding rows ch 5 to turn, d c in d c, ch 2, d c in next d c, repeat from *.

No. 11—Block or Solid Mesh (S M) Four double crochets form 1 solid mesh and 3 d c are required for each additional solid mesh. Open mesh and solid mesh are used in Filet Crochet.

No. 12—Slanting Shell St. Ch for desired length, work 2 d c in 4th st from hook, skip 3 sts, sl st in next st, * ch 3, 2 d c in same st with sl st, skip 3 sts, sl st in next st. Repeat from *. **2nd Row.** Ch 3, turn 2 d c in sl st, sl st in 3 ch loop of shell in previous row, * ch 3, 2 d c in same space, sl st in next shell, repeat from *.

No. 13—Bean or Pop Corn Stitch. Work 3 d c in same space, drop loop from hook insert hook in first d c made and draw loop through, ch 1 to tighten st.

No. 14—Cross Treble Crochet. Ch for desired length, thread over twice, insert in 5th st from hook, * work off two loops, thread over, skip 2 sts, insert in next st and work off all loops on needle 2 at a time, ch 2, d c in center to complete cross. Thread over twice, insert in next st and repeat from *.

No. 15—Cluster Stitch. Work 3 or 4 tr c in same st always retaining the last loop of each tr c on needle, thread over and pull through all loops on needle.

No. 16—Lacet St. Ch for desired length, work 1 s c in 10th st from hook, ch 3 skip 2 sts, 1 d c in next st, * ch 3, skip 2 sts, 1 s c in next st, ch 3, skip 2 sts 1 d c in next st, repeat from * to end of row, 2nd row, d c in d c, ch 5 d c in next d c.

No. 17—Knot Stitch (Sometimes Called Lovers Knot St.) Ch for desired length, * draw a ¼ inch loop on hook, thread over and pull through ch, s c in single loop of st, draw another ¼ inch loop, s c into loop, skip 4 sts, s c in next st, repeat from *. To turn make ⅜" knots, * s c in loop at right of s c and s c in loop at left of s c of previous row, 2 knot sts and repeat from *.

Metric Conversion Chart

CONVERTING INCHES TO CENTIMETERS AND YARDS TO METERS

mm — millimeters   cm — centimeters   m — meters

INCHES INTO MILLIMETERS AND CENTIMETERS
(Slightly rounded off for convenience)

inches	mm		cm	inches	cm	inches	cm	inches	cm
⅛	3mm			5	12.5	21	53.5	38	96.5
¼	6mm			5½	14	22	56	39	99
⅜	10mm	or	1cm	6	15	23	58.5	40	101.5
½	13mm	or	1.3cm	7	18	24	61	41	104
⅝	15mm	or	1.5cm	8	20.5	25	63.5	42	106.5
¾	20mm	or	2cm	9	23	26	66	43	109
⅞	22mm	or	2.2cm	10	25.5	27	68.5	44	112
1	25mm	or	2.5cm	11	28	28	71	45	114.5
1¼	32mm	or	3.2cm	12	30.5	29	73.5	46	117
1½	38mm	or	3.8cm	13	33	30	76	47	119.5
1¾	45mm	or	4.5cm	14	35.5	31	79	48	122
2	50mm	or	5cm	15	38	32	81.5	49	124.5
2½	65mm	or	6.5cm	16	40.5	33	84	50	127
3	75mm	or	7.5cm	17	43	34	86.5		
3½	90mm	or	9cm	18	46	35	89		
4	100mm	or	10cm	19	48.5	36	91.5		
4½	115mm	or	11.5cm	20	51	37	94		

YARDS TO METERS
(Slightly rounded off for convenience)

yards	meters	yards	meters	yards	meters	yards	meters	yards	meters
⅛	0.15	2⅛	1.95	4⅛	3.80	6⅛	5.60	8⅛	7.45
¼	0.25	2¼	2.10	4¼	3.90	6¼	5.75	8¼	7.55
⅜	0.35	2⅜	2.20	4⅜	4.00	6⅜	5.85	8⅜	7.70
½	0.50	2½	2.30	4½	4.15	6½	5.95	8½	7.80
⅝	0.60	2⅝	2.40	4⅝	4.25	6⅝	6.10	8⅝	7.90
¾	0.70	2¾	2.55	4¾	4.35	6¾	6.20	8¾	8.00
⅞	0.80	2⅞	2.65	4⅞	4.50	6⅞	6.30	8⅞	8.15
1	0.95	3	2.75	5	4.60	7	6.40	9	8.25
1⅛	1.05	3⅛	2.90	5⅛	4.70	7⅛	6.55	9⅛	8.35
1¼	1.15	3¼	3.00	5¼	4.80	7¼	6.65	9¼	8.50
1⅜	1.30	3⅜	3.10	5⅜	4.95	7⅜	6.75	9⅜	8.60
1½	1.40	3½	3.20	5½	5.05	7½	6.90	9½	8.70
1⅝	1.50	3⅝	3.35	5⅝	5.15	7⅝	7.00	9⅝	8.80
1¾	1.60	3¾	3.45	5¾	5.30	7¾	7.10	9¾	8.95
1⅞	1.75	3⅞	3.55	5⅞	5.40	7⅞	7.20	9⅞	9.05
2	1.85	4	3.70	6	5.50	8	7.35	10	9.15

AVAILABLE FABRIC WIDTHS

25"	65cm	50"	127cm
27"	70cm	54"/56"	140cm
35"/36"	90cm	58"/60"	150cm
39"	100cm	68"/70"	175cm
44"/45"	115cm	72"	180cm
48"	122cm		

AVAILABLE ZIPPER LENGTHS

4"	10cm	10"	25cm
5"	12cm	12"	30cm
6"	15cm	14"	35cm
7"	18cm	16"	40cm
8"	20cm	18"	45cm
9"	22cm	20"	50cm
22"	55cm		
24"	60cm		
26"	65cm		
28"	70cm		
30"	75cm		

Circular Double Ruffle

MATERIALS: J. & P. COATS OR CLARK'S O.N.T. BEST SIX CORD MERCERIZED CROCHET, *Size 30:* **Small Ball:** J. & P. COATS—*5 balls of White or Ecru, or 7 balls of any color, or* CLARK'S O.N.T.—*8 balls of White or Ecru, or 10 balls of any color.* **Big Ball:** J. & P. COATS—*3 balls of White, Ecru or Cream . . . Steel Crochet Hook No. 10.*

Doily measures 18 inches in diameter

Starting at center, ch 10. Join with sl st to form ring. **1st rnd:** 12 sc in ring. Sl st in first sc. **2nd rnd:** Ch 3, holding back on hook the last loop of each dc make 2 dc in same place as sl st, thread over and draw through all loops on hook (cluster made), * ch 3, make a 3-dc cluster in next sc. Repeat from * around. Join last ch-3 with sl st to tip of first cluster. **3rd rnd:** 5 sc in each sp around. Join. **4th rnd:** Sl st in next 3 sc, ch 3, make a 2-dc cluster in same place as last sl st, * ch 5, make a 3-dc cluster in center sc of next 5-sc group. Repeat from * around. Join. **5th rnd:** 7 sc in each loop around. Join. **6th rnd:** Sl st to center sc of first 7-sc group, ch 3 and complete a cluster as before, * ch 8, make a 3-dc cluster in center sc of next 7-sc group. Repeat from * around. Join. **7th rnd:** Ch 3, 13 dc in each loop around. Sl st in first dc (156 dc in the rnd). **8th rnd:** Ch 3 and complete a cluster as before, * ch 3, skip 3 dc, cluster in next dc. Repeat from * around. Join. **9th rnd:** 5 sc in each sp around. Join. **10th rnd:** Sl st to center sc of first 5-sc group, ch 3 and complete cluster as before in same place as last sl st, * ch 5, cluster in center sc of next 5-sc group. Repeat from * around. Join. **11th rnd:** 7 sc in each loop around. Join.

12th rnd: Sl st to center sc of first 7-sc group, ch 3 and complete cluster in same place as last sl st, * ch 7, cluster in center sc of next 7-sc group. Repeat from * around. Join. **13th rnd:** 9 sc in each loop around. Join. **14th rnd:** Sl st to center sc of first 9-sc group, ch 3 and complete cluster as before, * ch 7, cluster in center sc of next 9-sc group. Repeat from * around. Join. **15th rnd:** 9 sc in each loop around. Join. **16th rnd:** Ch 3 and complete cluster as before, * ch 4, cluster in center sc of next 9-sc group, ch 4, cluster in the sc over next cluster on 14th rnd. Repeat from * around. Join. **17th rnd:** Ch 3, make 6 dc in each sp around (468 dc). Sl st in first dc. **18th rnd:** Sc in same place as sl st, * ch 7, skip 4 dc, dc in next dc, (ch 3, skip next 3 dc, dc in next dc) 12 times; ch 7, skip 4 dc, sc in next dc. Repeat from * 3 more times; ** ch 7, skip 4 dc, dc in next dc, (ch 3, skip 3 dc, dc in next dc) 12 times; ch 7, skip 4 dc, sc in next 2 dc. Repeat from ** across remainder of rnd. Join. **19th rnd:** Sl st to center of next loop, sc in same loop, ch 7, sc in next loop, ch 7, dc in next loop, * (ch 3, dc in next loop) 9 times; (ch 7, sc in next loop) 4 times; ch 7, dc in next loop. Repeat from * around. Join. **20th rnd:** Sl st to center of next loop, sc in same loop, (ch 7, sc in next loop) twice; * ch 7, dc in next sp, (ch 3, dc in next sp) 6 times; (ch 7, sc in next loop) 7 times. Repeat from * around. Join. **21st rnd:** Sl st to center of next loop, sc in same loop, (ch 7, sc in next loop) 4 times; * ch 7, skip next dc, cluster in next dc, ch 7, skip next dc, sc in next sp, (ch 7, sc in next loop) 11 times. Repeat from * around. Join.

22nd rnd: Sl st to center of next loop, sc in same loop, (ch 7, sc in next loop) 3 times; * ch 7, cluster in next loop, ch 5, cluster in next loop, (ch 7, sc in next loop) 11 times. Repeat from * around. Join. **23rd rnd:** Sl st to center of next loop, sc in same loop, (ch 7, sc in next loop) twice; * ch 7, cluster in next loop, (ch 5, cluster in next loop) twice; (ch 7, sc in next loop) 10 times. Repeat from * around. Join. **24th rnd:** Sl st to center of next loop, sc in same loop, ch 7, sc in next loop, * ch 7, cluster in next loop, (ch 5, cluster in next loop) 3 times; (ch 7, sc in next loop) 9 times. Repeat from * around. Join. **25th rnd:** Sl st to center of next loop, sc in same loop, * ch 7, cluster in next loop, (ch 5, cluster in next loop) 4 times; (ch 7, sc in next loop) 8 times. Repeat from * around, ending with ch 3, tr in first sc. **26th rnd:** * Ch 7, cluster in next loop, (ch 5, cluster in next loop) 5 times; (ch 7, sc in next loop) 7 times. Repeat from * around, ending with ch 3, tr in tr. **27th rnd:** * Ch 7, cluster in next loop, (ch 5, cluster in next loop) 6 times; (ch 7, sc in next loop) 6 times. Repeat from * around, ending with ch 3, tr in tr. **28th rnd:** * (Ch 7, cluster in next loop) 8 times; (ch 7, sc in next loop) 5 times. Repeat from * around, ending with ch 3, tr in tr. **29th and 30th rnds:** * Ch 7, sc in next loop. Repeat from * around, ending with ch 3, tr in tr. **31st rnd:** * Ch 5, in next loop make sc, ch 5 and sc. Repeat from * around, ending with sc in last loop, ch 2, dc in tr. **32nd rnd:** * Ch 5, sc in next loop. Repeat from * around. Join last ch-5 with sl st in dc.

OUTER RUFFLE . . . 1st rnd: Ch 5, sc in next loop, * (ch 5, sc in same loop) twice; ch 5, sc in next loop. Repeat from * around. Join. **2nd to 5th rnds incl:** Sl st to center of next loop, ch 8, * dc in next loop, ch 5. Repeat from * around. Join last ch-5 with sl st to 3rd st of starting chain. **6th to 10th rnds incl:** Repeat 5th rnd, having ch-9 starting chain and ch-6 loops on 6th rnd, ch-10 starting chain and ch-7 loops on 7th rnd, ch-11 starting chain and ch-8 loops on 8th rnd, ch-12 starting chain and ch-9 loops on 9th rnd and ch-13 starting chain and ch-10 loops on 10th rnd. Break off.

INNER RUFFLE . . . 1st rnd: Attach thread to any dc on the solid dc rnd (17th rnd), sc in same dc, * ch 5, skip 1 dc, sc in next dc. Repeat from * around. Join. **2nd to 7th rnds incl:** Work exactly as for 2nd to 7th rnds incl of Outer Ruffle. Break off. Starch lightly and press. ✿

Easter Lily

MATERIALS: J. & P. Coats or Clark's O.N.T. Best Six Cord Mercerized Crochet, Size 30: **Small Ball:** J. & P. Coats—3 balls of White or Ecru, or 4 balls of any color, or Clark's O.N.T.—5 balls of White or Ecru, or 6 balls of any color . . . Steel Crochet Hook No. 10.

Doily measures 14 inches in diameter

Starting at center, ch 10. Join with sl st to form ring. **1st rnd:** Ch 3, 2 dc in ring, (ch 3, 3 dc in ring) 7 times; ch 3, sl st in 3rd ch of ch-3. **2nd rnd:** Ch 3, dc in next 2 dc, * in next sp make dc, ch 3 and dc; dc in next 3 dc. Repeat from * around, ending with dc, ch 3 and dc in last sp. Sl st in top of starting chain. **3rd rnd:** Ch 3, * in next dc make dc, ch 5 and dc; dc in next 2 dc, in next sp make dc, ch 3 and dc; dc in next 2 dc. Repeat from * around. Join. **4th rnd:** Sl st in next 3 dc and in next 2 ch, sc in same loop, * ch 5, holding back on hook the last loop of each tr make 2 tr in next sp, thread over and draw through all loops on hook (cluster made), ch 5, cluster in same place, ch 5, sc in next loop. Repeat from * around. Join. **5th rnd:** Sl st in next 5 ch, sl st in tip of next cluster, ch 4, tr in same place, * ch 3, in next sp make cluster, ch 5 and cluster; ch 3, cluster in tip of next cluster, ch 5, cluster in tip of next cluster. Repeat from * around. Join.

6th rnd: Ch 4, tr in same place, cluster in tip of next cluster, * ch 5, (cluster in tip of next cluster) twice; ch 5, tr in next sp, ch 5, (cluster in tip of next cluster) twice. Repeat from * around. Join. **7th rnd:** Sl st in next cluster, ch 4, tr in same place, skip next cluster, cluster in tip of next cluster, * ch 3, tr in next sp, ch 5, 5 tr in next tr, ch 5, tr in next sp, ch 3, (skip next cluster, tr in tip of next cluster) twice. Repeat from * around. Join.

8th rnd: Sl st in next 3 ch, sl st in next tr, ch 7, * 2 tr in next tr, tr in next 3 tr, 2 tr in next tr, ch 3, tr in next tr, ch 3, thread over twice; (insert hook in next sp and draw loop through) twice and complete as for a tr; ch 3, tr in next tr, ch 3. Repeat from * around. Join. **9th rnd:** Ch 4, * 2 tr in next tr, tr in next 2 tr, in next tr make tr, ch 10 and tr; tr in next 2 tr, tr in next tr, tr in next tr, (ch 5, tr in next tr) twice. Repeat from * around. Join. **10th rnd:** Sl st in next tr, ch 4, tr in same tr, * tr in next 3 tr, ch 10, sc in next loop, ch 10, skip next tr, tr in next 3 tr, 2 tr in next tr, ch 10, skip next tr, sc in next tr, ch 10, skip next tr, 2 tr in next tr. Repeat from * around. Join. **11th rnd:** Ch 4, tr in same place as sl st, * tr in next 3 tr, (ch 10, sc in next loop) twice; ch 10, skip next tr, tr in next 3 tr, 2 tr in next tr, sc in next loop,

ch 10, sc in next loop, 2 tr in next tr. Repeat from * around, ending with sc in last loop. Join. **12th rnd:** Ch 4, tr in same place, * tr in next 3 tr, (ch 10, sc in next loop) 3 times; ch 10, skip next tr, tr in next 3 tr, 2 tr in next tr, sc in next loop, 2 tr in next tr. Repeat from * around. Join. **13th rnd:** Ch 4, holding back on hook the last loop of each tr make tr in next 3 tr, thread over and draw through all loops on hook, * (ch 10, sc in next loop) 4 times; ch 10, skip next tr, holding back on hook the last loop of each tr make tr in next 4 tr, in the next sc and in the following 4 tr, thread over and draw through all loops on hook (cluster made). Repeat from * around, ending with a 5-tr cluster made over last 4 tr and the following sc. Join. **14th rnd:** Sl st to center of next loop, ch 14, * tr in next loop, ch 10. Repeat from * around. Join with sl st to 4th ch of ch-14. **15th rnd:** Ch 4, make 11 tr in each loop around. Join.

RUFFLE . . . 1st rnd: Ch 9, * skip 1 tr, tr in next tr, ch 5. Repeat from * around. Join. **2nd, 3rd and 4th rnds:** Sl st to center of next loop, ch 9, * tr in next loop, ch 5. Repeat from * around. Join. **5th to 8th rnds incl:** Repeat 2nd rnd, having one additional chain on loops of each following rnd. Break off at end of 8th rnd. Starch lightly and press. ✣

Victorian Ruffle

Materials Required: AMERICAN THREAD COMPANY "DE LUXE" MERCERIZED CROCHET AND KNITTING COTTON, ARTICLE 346

7—300 yd. Balls White.

Steel Crochet Hook No. 7.

Doily measures about 25½ x 31 inches without ruffle.

Ch 39, d c in 7th st from hook, * ch 1, skip 1 st of ch, d c in next st, repeat from * 15 times.

2nd Row. S c into last mesh over the d c just made, * ch 25, s c in same mesh, repeat from * 6 times, ch 20, 2 s c in each of the next 7 meshes, ch 20, s c in next mesh, * ch 25, s c in same mesh, repeat from * 3 times, ch 20, 2 s c in each of the next 7 meshes, ch 20, s c in corner mesh, * ch 25, s c in same mesh, repeat from * 7 times, ch 20 and working on other side of meshes, work 2 s c in each of the next 7 meshes, ch 20, s c in next mesh, * ch 25, s c in same mesh, repeat from * 3 times, ch 20, 2 s c in each of the next 7 meshes, ch 20, s c in next mesh (corner) ch 25, s c in same mesh, break thread.

3rd Row. Attach thread in 1st loop of center group on side, s c in same space, * ch 7, s c in next loop, repeat from * 4 times, s c in 1st loop of end group, * ch 7, s c in next loop, repeat from * 8 times, s c in 1st loop of next group at side, * ch 7, s c in next loop, repeat from * 4 times, s c in 1st loop of end group, * ch 7, s c in next loop, repeat from * 8 times, join to 1st s c.

4th Row. Sl st to center of loop, * ch 10, s c in next loop, repeat from * all around, then without joining rows work 3 more rows of 10 ch loops.

Next Row. * Ch 30, s c in same loop, repeat from * 5 times, 10 s c in next loop, s c in next loop and work 6-30 ch loops in same loop, repeat from * all around, join and break thread. Attach thread in 1st long loop and work 10 ch loops over long loops and 3 ch loops between groups of long loops. Sl st to center of loop and work a 10 ch loop in each 10 ch loop. Without joining rows work 8 more rows of 10 ch loops.

Next Row. Ch 3, work 5 d c in same loop, * ch 5, 5 d c in next loop, repeat from * all around.

SCALLOP: Sl st into loop, * ch 10, s c in same loop, ch 10, s c in same loop, ch 10, s c in same loop, ch 10, s c in next loop, repeat from * all around and continue work without joining rows.

Next Row. * Ch 10, s c in next loop, repeat from * all around and repeat the last row 12 times, break thread. ✽

Whirlpool

MATERIALS: J. & P. Coats or Clark's O.N.T. Best Six Cord Mercerized Crochet, *Size 30:* **Small Ball:** J. & P. Coats—6 balls of White or Ecru, or 8 balls of any color, or Clark's O.N.T.—8 balls of White or Ecru, or 11 balls of any color. **Big Ball:** J. & P. Coats—3 balls of White, Ecru or Cream . . . Steel Crochet Hook No. 10.

Doily measures 21 inches in diameter

Starting at center, ch 8. Join with sl st to form ring. **1st rnd:** Ch 1, 13 sc in ring. Sl st in first sc. **2nd rnd:** Sc in same place as sl st, * ch 3, sc in next sc. Repeat from * around, ending with ch 3, sl st in first sc (13 loops). **3rd and 4th rnds:** Sl st in next ch, sc in same loop, * ch 3, sc in next loop. Repeat from * around. Join. **5th rnd:** Sl st in next ch, sc in same loop, * ch 4, sc in next loop. Repeat from * around. Join. **6th rnd:** Sl st in next 2 ch, sc in same loop, * ch 5, sc in next loop. Repeat from * around. Join. **7th rnd:** Sl st in next 2 ch, sl st in same loop, ch 6, dc in same loop, * ch 3, in next loop make dc, ch 3 and dc. Repeat from * around. Join last ch 3 to 3rd ch of ch-6. **8th and 9th rnds:** Sl st in next ch, sc in same loop, * ch 5, sc in next loop. Repeat from * around. Join. **10th rnd:** Sl st in next 2 ch, sc in same loop, * ch 6, sc in next loop. Repeat from * around. Join. **11th rnd:** Sl st in next 2 ch, sl st in same loop, ch 10, * dc in next loop, ch 7. Repeat from * around. Join last ch 7 to 3rd ch of ch-10. **12th rnd:** Sl st in next 2 ch, sc in same loop, ch 5, sc in same loop, * ch 5, in next loop make sc, ch 5 and sc. Repeat from * around. Join. **13th rnd:** Sl st to center of next loop, sc in same loop, ch 11, * skip next loop, dc in next loop, ch 8. Repeat from * around. Join. **14th rnd:** Sl st in next ch, sc in same loop, ch 7, sc in same loop, * ch 7, in next loop make sc, ch 7 and sc. Repeat from * around. Join. **15th and 16th rnds:** Sl st to center of next loop, sc in same loop, * ch 7, sc in next loop. Repeat from * around. Join. **17th rnd:** Sl st in next 3 ch, sl st in same loop, ch 8, * dc in next loop, ch 5. Repeat from * around. Join last ch 5 to 3rd ch of ch-8. **18th rnd:** Sl st in next ch, sc in same loop, ch 5, sc in same loop, * ch 5, in next loop make sc, ch 5 and sc. Repeat from * around. Join.

19th rnd: Sl st in next 2 ch and in same loop, ch 10, * skip next loop, dc in next loop, ch 7. Repeat from * around. Join last ch 7 with sl st to 3rd ch of ch-10. **20th rnd:** Sl st in next ch, sc in same loop, ch 6, sc in same loop, * ch 6, in next loop make sc, ch 6 and sc. Repeat from * around. Join. **21st rnd:** Sl st in next 3 ch and in same loop, ch 12, * skip next loop, tr in next loop, ch 8. Repeat from * around. Join. **22nd rnd:** Sl st in next 2 ch, sc in same loop, ch 5, sc in same loop, * ch 5, in next loop make sc, ch 5 and sc. Repeat from * around. Join. **23rd, 24th and 25th rnds:** Sl st in next 2 ch, sc in same loop, * ch 5, sc in next loop. Repeat from * around. Join. **26th rnd:** Repeat 17th rnd. **27th rnd:** Repeat 18th rnd, making ch-4 (instead of ch-5) loops. **28th rnd:** Sl st in next 2 ch, sl st in same loop, ch 8, * skip next loop, dc in next loop, ch 5. Repeat from * around. Join. **29th rnd:** Repeat 18th rnd. **30th and 31st rnds:** Repeat 28th and 29th rnds. **32nd rnd:** Repeat 28th rnd, making ch 6 (instead of ch-5) between dc's. **33rd rnd:** Sl st in next 2 ch, in same loop make sc, ch 5 and sc; * ch 5, in next loop make sc, ch 5 and sc. Repeat from * around. Join. **34th to 37th rnds incl:** Sl st to center of next loop, sc in same loop, * ch 5, sc in next loop. Repeat from * around. Join. **38th rnd:** Sl st to center of next loop, ch 6, * dc in next loop, ch 3. Repeat from * around. Join. **39th rnd:** Sl st in next ch, in same loop make sc, ch 3 and sc; * ch 3, in next loop make sc, ch 3 and sc. Repeat from * around. Join. **40th rnd:** Sl st in next ch, sl st in same loop, ch 6, * skip next loop, dc in next loop, ch 3. Repeat from * around. Join. **41st to 46th rnds incl:** Repeat 39th and 40th rnds alternately, having ch 4 (instead of ch-3) on 44th rnd. **47th rnd:** Repeat 39th rnd.

OUTER RUFFLE . . . 1st rnd: Sc in next loop, * ch 5, sc in same loop, ch 5, sc in next loop. Repeat from * around. Join. **2nd to 5th rnds incl:** Sl st to center of next loop, ch 8, * dc in next loop, ch 5. Repeat from * around. Join last ch 5 with sl st to 3rd st of starting chain. **6th to 10th rnds incl:** Repeat 5th rnd, having ch-9 starting chain and ch-6 loops on 6th rnd, ch-10 starting chain and ch-7 loops on 7th rnd, ch-11 starting chain and ch-8 loops on 8th rnd, ch-12 starting chain and ch-9 loops on 9th rnd and ch-13 starting chain and ch-10 loops on 10th rnd. Break off.

INNER RUFFLE . . . Attach thread to a loop on 25th rnd, and work exactly as for Outer Ruffle until 7th rnd is completed. Break off. Starch lightly and press. ✿

Waterfall

MATERIALS: J. & P. Coats or Clark's O.N.T. Best Six Cord Mercerized Crochet, *Size 30:* **Small Ball:** J. & P. Coats—*8 balls of White or Ecru, or 11 balls of any color,* or Clark's O.N.T.—*12 balls of White or Ecru, or 16 balls of any color . . .* Steel Crochet Hook No. 10.

Doily measures 20 inches in diameter

Starting at center, ch 9. Join with sl st to form ring. **1st rnd:** (Ch 7, 4 sc in ring) 4 times. Do not join rnds unless specified. **2nd rnd:** * Ch 7, 4 sc in next loop, sc in next 2 sc. Repeat from * around. **3rd to 19th rnds incl:** * Ch 7, 4 sc in next loop, sc in each sc to within last 2 sc of sc group. Repeat from * around (40 sc in each group on 19th rnd). **20th rnd:** * Ch 7, sc in next loop, (ch 7, skip 3 sc, sc in next sc) 9 times. Repeat from * around (40 loops). **21st rnd:** * Ch 7, sc in next loop. Repeat from * around, ending with sl st in first sc. **22nd to 25th rnds incl:** Sl st to center of next loop, sc in same loop, * ch 8, sc in next loop. Repeat from * around. Join as before. **26th rnd:** Sl st to center of next loop, ch 12, * tr in next loop, ch 8. Repeat from * around. Join to 4th ch of ch-12. **27th rnd:** Sc in same place as sl st, * 9 sc in next sp, sc in next tr. Repeat from * around. Join. **28th rnd:** Sc in same place as sl st, * ch 7, skip 4 sc, sc in back loop of next sc. Repeat from * around. Join. **29th to 32nd rnds incl:** Sl st to center of next loop, sc in same loop, * ch 7, sc in next loop. Repeat from * around. Join. **33rd to 37th rnds incl:** Sl st to center of next loop, sc in same loop, * ch 8, sc in next loop. Repeat from * around. Join. **38th rnd:** Repeat 26th rnd. **39th rnd:** Repeat 27th rnd.

RUFFLE . . . 1st rnd: * Ch 5, sc in next sc. Repeat from * around, ending with ch 2, dc at base of first loop. **2nd to 6th rnds incl:** * Ch 6, sc in next loop. Repeat from * around, ending with ch 3, dc in dc. **7th rnd:** * Ch 7, sc in next loop. Repeat from * around, ending with ch 3, tr in dc. **8th to 12th rnds incl:** * Ch 7, sc in next loop. Repeat from * around, ending with ch 3, tr in tr. **13th to 18th rnds incl:** * Ch 8, sc in next loop. Repeat from * around, ending with ch 4, tr in tr. Break off.

SMALL RUFFLE . . . 1st rnd: Attach thread to front loop of any sc on 28th rnd, * ch 5, sc in front loop of next sc. Repeat from * around. Work as for Large Ruffle until 12 rnds are completed. Join and break off. Starch lightly and press. ✿

Daffodil Frill

MATERIALS—1-ball Mercerized Crochet Cotton, size 50, in White, Cream, Ecru or a color. Crochet hook, size 14.

Ch 10, sl st in 1st st. Ch 11, dtr in ring, (ch 3, dtr in ring) 12 times, ch 3, sl st in 8th st of 1st 11-ch.

2nd Row. Ch 3, (4 dc in next sp, 1 dc in dtr) repeated around. Sl st in 1st 3-ch and in next 2 dc.

3rd Row. Ch 1, sc in next dc, (ch 7, sk 3 dc, sc in next 2 dc) 13 times, ch 3, dc in 1st 1-ch.

4th Row. Ch 8, turn, 5 dtr in dc, (ch 6, 6 dtr in center st of next lp) repeated around. Ch 3, dc in 1st 8-ch.

5th Row. Turn, 2 dc in last dtr, * 1 tr in next dtr, 2 tr in next, ch 5, sl st in last tr for a p, 2 tr in next dtr, 1 tr in next, 2 dc in next, sc in 6-ch lp, 2 dc in next dtr. Repeat from * around.

6th Row. Sl st to 3d st from p, ch 12, dc in 3d tr to left of next p, * ch 9, dc in 3d tr before next p, ch 9, dc in 3d tr to left of same p. Repeat from * around. End with 4-ch, tr in 3d st of 1st 12-ch.

7th Row. (Ch 13, sc in next lp) repeated around with ch 6 and dtr for final lp.

8th Row. Repeat Row 4.

9th Row. Repeat Row 5 except make only 1 dc in 1st and last dtr of each pattern.

10th Row. Repeat Row 6.

11th–13th Rows. Repeat Row 7.

14th Row. * Dtr in 7th st of next lp, (ch 1, dtr) 9 times in same st, sc in next lp. Repeat from * around.

15th Row. Sl st to 1st 1-ch sp, * (ch 6, sc in next sp) 8 times, ch 6, sc in 1st sp on next shell. Repeat from * around, with 3-ch and dc for end lp.

16th Row. Turn, (ch 7, sc in next lp) repeated around, with 3-ch and dc for end lp.

17th Row. Turn and make 9-ch lps around with 4-ch and tr for end lp.

18th Row. Turn, 11-ch lps around, 5-ch and dtr for end lp.

19th Row. Turn, 12-ch lps, 6-ch and tr for end lp.

20th Row. Turn, 13-ch lps, 6-ch and dtr for end lp.

21st Row. Turn, 14-ch lps, 7-ch and dtr for end lp.

22nd Row. Turn, 15-ch lps, 7-ch and dtr for end lp.

23rd Row. Repeat Row 22.

24th Row. Turn, 16-ch lps, 8-ch and dtr for end lp.

25th–27th Rows. Repeat Row 24.

28th Row. Without turning, * ch 6, sc in next lp, ch 12, a 3-tr-Cluster in 8th st of next lp, ch 7, sc in 5th ch st from hook for a p, ch 3, a 3-tr-Cluster in next st on same lp, ch 12, sc in next lp. Repeat from * around. Fasten off.

Dip Doily in hot, cooked starch (about 2 tsps. starch in 1 cup water). Roll in a cloth to absorb excess. Stretch and iron ruffle until partly stiffened. Pin down center to keep it flat, arrange ruffle in even ripples and let dry. ✺

Rose Ruffle

**Materials Required: AMERICAN THREAD COMPANY
"STAR" MERCERIZED CROCHET COTTON, ARTICLE 30
Size 30**

4—65 yd. Balls Shaded Green or any Color desired or
1—250 yd. Ball.
Steel Crochet Hook No. 12.
Doily measures about 5 inches in diameter without ruffle.

Ch 8, join to form a ring, ch 3 and work 14 d c in ring,
join in 3rd st of ch.

2nd Row. Ch 5, d c in next d c, * ch 2, d c in next d c, repeat
from * 12 times, ch 2, join in 3rd st of ch.

3rd Row. Sl st to loop, ch 3, 2 d c in same space, * ch 1, 3 d c
in next loop, repeat from * all around, ch 1, join in 3rd
st of ch.

4th Row. S c over last ch 1 made, * ch 7, s c over next ch 1,
repeat from * 13 times, ch 3, tr c in 1st s c, this brings
thread in position for next row.

5th Row. S c in same space, * ch 9, s c in next loop, repeat
from * all around ending row with ch 5, d tr c (3 times
over needle) in 1st s c.

6th Row. Ch 4, 5 tr c in same loop, * s c in next loop, ch 11,
s c in next loop, 11 tr c in next loop, repeat from * 3 times,
s c in next loop, ch 11, s c in next loop, 5 tr c in next loop,
join in 4th st of ch.

7th Row. S c in same space, * ch 9, d c in next s c, ch 9, s c
in next loop, ch 9, d c in next s c, ch 9, s c in center st of
next tr c group, repeat from * all around in same manner
ending row with ch 5, d tr c in 1st s c.

8th Row. S c in same loop, * ch 11, s c in next loop, repeat
from * all around, join.

9th Row. Work 11 s c over each loop, join.

10th Row. Ch 5, skip 1 s c, d c in next s c, * ch 1, skip 1 s c,
d c in next s c, repeat from * all around ending row with
ch 1, join in 3rd st of ch.

11th Row. Work 2 s c in each mesh, join.

12th Row. S c in same space, * ch 9, skip 4 s c, s c in next
s c, repeat from * all around ending row with ch 5, d tr c
in 1st s c.

13th Row. * Ch 9, s c in next loop, repeat from * all around
ending row with ch 5, d tr c in d tr c.

14th Row. * Ch 7, s c in next loop, repeat from * all around
ending row with ch 1, tr tr c (4 times over needle) in d tr c.

15th Row. * Ch 10, s c in same loop, repeat from * twice,
ch 10, s c in next loop, repeat from beginning all around
in same manner ending row with ch 5, d tr c in tr tr c.

16th and 17th Rows. Ch 10, s c in next loop, repeat from
beginning all around ending each row with ch 5, d tr c
in d tr c.

18th Row. 4 s c in same loop, 7 s c in each of the following
loops ending row with 4 s c in 1st loop, join.

19th Row. Ch 5, skip 2 s c, d c in next s c, * ch 2, skip 2 s c,
d c in next s c, repeat from * all around, ch 2, join in 3rd
st of ch.

20th Row. 2 s c in each of the 1st 9 meshes, 3 s c in each
remaining mesh, join.

21st Row. S c in same space, * ch 11, skip 5 s c, s c in next
s c, repeat from * all around ending row with ch 7, tr c
in 1st s c.

22nd Row. 6 tr c in next loop, ch 5, sl st in last tr c for picot,
5 tr c in same space, s c in next loop, ch 10, sl st in 6th st
from hook for picot, ch 4, s c in next loop, repeat from
beginning all around, join, break thread. ✤

Footloose

Materials Required: AMERICAN THREAD COMPANY "GEM" MERCERIZED CROCHET COTTON, ARTICLE 35 Size 30

3—350 yd. Balls White or Ecru.

Steel Crochet Hook No. 12.

16 Motifs 4 x 4 are required for doily measuring 7½ x 7½ inches without ruffle.

Ch 5, join to form a ring, s c in ring, * ch 4, s c in ring, repeat from * 6 times, ch 1, d c in 1st s c (this brings thread in position for next row.)

2nd Row. Ch 7, * thread over needle twice, insert in 5th st from hook, pull through and work off 2 loops twice, repeat from * once, thread over and pull through all loops on needle at one time, * d c in next loop, cluster st in top of d c just made, (cluster st: ch 4, this counts as 1 tr c, thread over twice, insert in st, pull through and work off 2 loops twice, thread over twice, insert in same space, pull through and work off 2 loops twice, thread over and pull through all loops at one time) repeat from * all around, join at base of 1st cluster st.

3rd Row. Cluster st in same space, ch 3, 3 tr c cluster st in same space, * ch 9, s c in d c between next 2 cluster sts, ch 9, 2-3 tr c cluster sts in d c between next 2 cluster sts with ch 3 between, repeat from * twice, ch 9, s c in d c between next 2 cluster sts, ch 9, join in top of 1st cluster st.

4th Row. Sl st to center st of ch 3 loop, s c in same space, * ch 9, s c in next loop, cluster st in s c just made, cluster st in top of cluster st just made, s c in next loop, ch 9, s c in next ch 3 loop, repeat from * twice, ch 9, s c in next loop, cluster st in s c just made, cluster st in cluster st, s c in next loop, ch 5, d tr c (3 times over needle) in 1st s c.

5th Row. Ch 7, 2 d tr c with ch 9 between in same space as d tr c just made, * ch 7, s c in next loop, ch 7, s c between next 2 cluster sts, ch 7, s c in next loop, ch 7, 2 d tr c with ch 9 between in next s c, repeat from * twice, ch 7, s c in next loop, ch 7, s c between next 2 cluster sts, ch 7, sl st in 1st d tr c, break thread.

Work another motif in same manner joining to 1st motif in last row as follows: ch 7, d tr c in same space as d tr c just made, ch 4, sl st in center st of corner loop of 1st motif, ch 4, d tr c in same space with last d tr c of 2nd motif, ch 3, join to center st of next loop of 1st motif, ch 3, s c in next loop of 2nd motif, ch 3, join to center st of next loop of 1st motif, ch 3, s c between next 2 cluster sts of 2nd motif, ch 3, join to center st of next loop of 1st motif, ch 3, s c in next loop of 2nd motif, ch 3, join to center st of next loop of 1st motif, ch 3, d tr c in next s c of 2nd motif, ch 4, join to center st of corner loop of 1st motif, ch 4, complete motif in same manner as 1st motif. Join 3rd motif to 2nd motif and 4th motif to 1st and 3rd motifs in same manner.

RUFFLE: Attach thread in any corner loop, s c in same space, * ch 10, s c in same loop, repeat from * 5 times, * ch 10, s c in next loop, ch 10, s c in same loop, ch 10, s c in same loop, repeat from * across side to next corner, ch 10, s c in corner loop, * ch 10, s c in same loop, repeat from * 5 times, continue all around in same manner working other corners same as last corner ending row with ch 5, tr tr c (4 times over needle) in 1st s c, this brings thread in position for next row.

Next 2 Rows. Ch 10, s c in next loop, repeat from beginning all around ending each row with ch 5, tr tr c in tr tr c.

4th Row. S c in same space, ** cluster st in s c just made, cluster st in top of cluster st just made, s c in next loop, * ch 10, s c in next loop, repeat from * twice, repeat from ** all around ending row with ch 5, tr tr c in tr tr c.

5th Row. Ch 10, * thread over twice, insert in 5th st from hook, thread over and work off 2 loops twice, repeat from

*, thread over and work off all loops at one time, sl st in space between next 2 cluster sts, cluster st in same space, ch 5, s c in next loop, * ch 10, s c in next loop, repeat from * once, repeat from beginning all around ending row with ch 5, tr tr c in tr tr c.

6th Row. * Ch 10, s c in next loop, repeat from * twice, cluster st in last s c, cluster st in top of cluster st just made, s c in next loop, repeat from beginning all around in same manner ending row with sl st in tr tr c.

7th Row. Sl st to center of next loop, s c in same space, ** ch 10, s c in next loop, ch 10, s c in next loop, ch 10, *

thread over twice, insert in 5th st from hook, thread over and work off 2 loops twice, repeat from * once, thread over and work off all loops at one time, sl st in space between next 2 cluster sts, cluster st in same space, ch 5, s c in next loop, repeat from ** all around omitting ch 5 at end of row, tr tr c in 1st s c.

8th Row. S c in same space, * cluster st in same space, ch 5, sl st in 5th st from hook for picot, cluster st in top of cluster st, s c in next loop, ch 10, sl st in 6th st from hook for picot, ch 4, s c in next loop, repeat from * all around, ending row with sl st, break thread. ❁

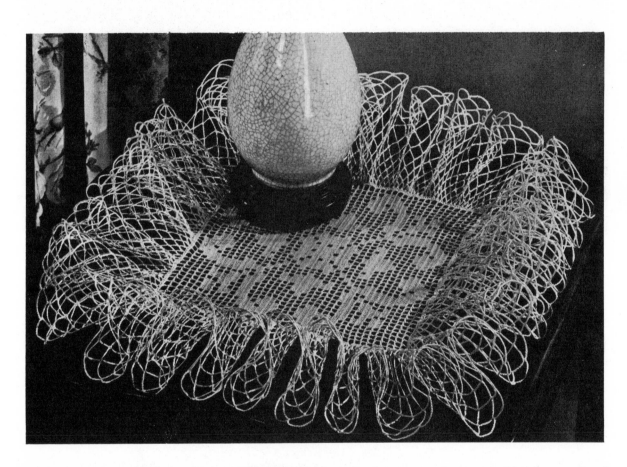

Fancy-Free

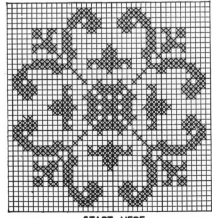

START HERE

MATERIALS: J. & P. Coats or Clark's O.N.T. Best Six Cord Mercerized Crochet, *Size 30:* **Small Ball:** J. & P. Coats—*3 balls of White, Ecru or any color,* or Clark's O.N.T. —*4 balls of White or Ecru, or 5 balls of any color* . . . Steel Crochet Hook No. 10.

Doily measures 12 inches square (including ruffle)

GAUGE: 5 sps make 1 inch; 5 rows make 1 inch.

NOTE: bl .... Block

Starting at bottom of chart, make a chain 10 inches long (15 ch sts to 1 inch). **1st row:** Dc in 8th ch from hook (sp made), * ch 2, skip 2 ch, dc in next ch (another sp made). Repeat from * across, until 41 sps in all are made. Cut off remaining chain. Ch 5, turn. **2nd row:** Skip first dc, dc in next dc (sp made over sp), ch 2, dc in next dc (another sp made over sp), make 12 more sps, 2 dc in next sp, dc in next dc (bl made over sp), make 2 more bls, 7 sps, 3 bls, 14 sps. Ch 5, turn. **3rd row:** 13 sps, 1 bl, dc in next 3 dc (bl made over bl), make 3 more bls, 5 sps, 5 bls, 13 sps. Ch 5, turn. **4th row:** 12 sps, 3 bls, ch 2, skip 2 dc, dc in next dc (sp made over bl), 3 bls, 3 sps, 3 bls, 1 sp, 3 bls, 12 sps. Ch 5, turn.

Starting with the 5th row follow chart to top. Do not break off but work all around as follows:

RUFFLE . . . 1st rnd: Sc closely around. Join. **2nd rnd:** Sc in same place as sl st, * ch 5, skip 1 sc, sc in next sc. Repeat from * around, ending with ch 5, sl st in first sc. **3rd rnd:** Sl st to center of next loop, sc in same loop, * ch 6, sc in next loop. Repeat from * around. Join. **4th to 13th rnds incl:** Repeat 3rd rnd, having 1 additional ch on loops of each rnd. Break off at end of 13th rnd. Starch lightly and press. ❁

Fairy Frosting

Shown in color on the front cover.

MATERIALS: J. & P. Coats or Clark's O.N.T. Best Six Cord Mercerized Crochet, *Size 20:* **Small Ball:** J. & P. Coats—*10 balls of White or Ecru,* or Clark's O.N.T.—*15 balls of White or Ecru . . .* Steel Crochet Hook No. 9.

Oval Doily measures 16 x 20 inches; Each small doily measures 10 inches in diameter

OVAL DOILY—First Motif . . . Starting at center, ch 8. Join with sl st to form ring. **1st rnd:** Ch 5, (dc in ring, ch 2) 11 times. Join last ch-2 with sl st in 3rd st of starting chain. **2nd rnd:** Ch 4, * 3 tr in next sp, tr in next dc. Repeat from * around, ending with 3 tr in last sp. Join with sl st to top of ch-4. **3rd rnd:** Ch 1, sc in same place as sl st, * ch 5, skip next tr, sc in next tr. Repeat from * around, ending with ch 2, dc in first sc made. **4th rnd:** * Ch 5, sc in next loop. Repeat from * around, ending with ch 2, dc in dc. **5th rnd:** * Ch 10, skip 1 loop, sc in next loop. Repeat from * around, joining last ch-10 with sl st in dc. **6th rnd:** In each ch-10 loop make 6 sc. **7th rnd:** Sl st in next 6 sc, sl st in next loop, ch 4 (to count as tr), holding back on hook the last loop of each tr make 2 tr in same loop, thread over and draw through all loops on hook (cluster made), * (ch 7, make a 3-tr cluster

in same loop) **twice;** 3-tr cluster in next loop. Repeat from * around, joining last cluster with sl st in tip of first cluster. **8th rnd:** Sl st in next 3 ch, ch 1, sc in same loop, * ch 10, sc in next loop. Repeat from * around, joining last ch-10 with sl st in first sc made. Break off.

SECOND MOTIF . . . Work as for First Motif until 7th rnd is completed. **8th rnd:** Sl st in next 3 ch, ch 1, sc in same loop, (ch 5, sc in corresponding loop on First Motif, ch 5, sc in next loop on Second Motif) 3 times and complete as for First Motif.

THIRD MOTIF . . . Work as for First Motif until 7th rnd is completed. **8th rnd:** Sl st in next 3 ch, ch 1, sc in same loop, ch 5, sc in 3rd loop preceding joining on First Motif, ch 5, sc in next loop on Third Motif, (ch 5, sc in next loop on First Motif, (ch 5, sc in next loop on Third Motif) twice; (ch 5, sc in next free loop on Second Motif, ch 5, sc in next loop on Third Motif) 3 times and complete rnd as for First Motif.

FOURTH MOTIF . . . Work as for First Motif, joining 3 loops of this motif to Second and Third Motifs as before.

Now work all around outer edges of motifs as follows: **1st rnd:** Skip first free loop following any joining, attach

thread to next loop, sc in same place, * ch 10, sc in next loop. Repeat from * around, skipping the loop immediately preceding and the loop immediately following each joining. Join last ch-10 with sl st to first sc. **2nd and 3rd rnds:** Sl st to center of next loop, sc in same loop, * ch 10, sc in next loop. Repeat from * around, skipping the loop directly above each joining.

RUFFLE . . . 1st rnd: Make 10 sc in each loop around. Sl st in first sc. **2nd rnd:** Ch 1, sc in same place as sl st, * ch 5, sc in next sc. Repeat from * around. Join last ch-5 with sl st to first sc. **3rd rnd:** Sl st to center of next loop, sc in same loop, * ch 5, sc in next loop. Repeat from * around. Join. **4th to 11th rnds incl:** Repeat 3rd rnd, making ch-6 loops on 4th, 5th and 6th rnds and having 1 more ch on loops of each following rnd. Break off.

SMALL DOILY . . . Make motif as for Oval Doily. Do not break off but work all around outer edges as follows: **1st rnd:** Sl st to center of next loop, sc in same loop, * ch 10, sc in next loop. Repeat from * around. Join. **2nd and 3rd rnds:** Make ch-10 loops around.

RUFFLE . . . Work as for Ruffle of Oval Doily. Starch lightly and press. ❉

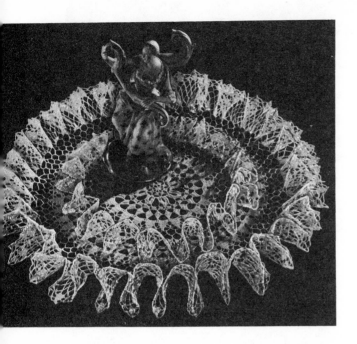

Aurora Borealis

Approximate Size 12 inches in diameter without Ruffle
This doily can be made with the following:
"GEM" CROCHET COTTON, Article 35, size 20
2 balls White or
"STAR" CROCHET COTTON, Article 20, size 20
3 balls White
Steel crochet hook No. 11

Ch 5, join to form a ring, ch 1 and work 8 s c in ring, join in 1st s c.

2nd Round—Ch 6, d c in next s c, * ch 3, d c in next s c, repeat from * 5 times, ch 3, join in 3rd st of ch.

3rd Round—Sl st into loop, ch 3, 2 d c in same space, * ch 5, 3 d c in next loop, repeat from * all around, ch 5, join in 3rd st of ch.

4th Round—Sl st to center st of next loop, ch 14, sl st in same space, * ch 7, sl st in center st of next loop, ch 14, sl st in same space, repeat from * all around, ch 7, join in last sl st.

5th Round—Sl st in 1st st of ch 14 loop, ch 3 and work 10 d c over loop, ch 3, 10 d c over same loop, d c in last st of same ch 14 loop, sl st in center st of next ch 7 loop, * d c in 1st st of next ch 14 loop, 10 d c over loop, ch 3, 10 d c over same loop, d c in last st of same ch 14 loop, sl st in center st of next ch 7 loop, repeat from * all around, join in 3rd st of ch.

6th Round—Sl st to 6th d c, ch 8, * sl st in loop at top of scallop, ch 3, sl st in same space, ch 5, skip 4 d c on opposite side of same scallop, d c in next d c, ch 5, d c in 7th d c on right hand side of next scallop, ch 5, repeat from * all around ending with sl st in loop at top of next scallop, ch 3, sl st in same space, ch 5, skip 4 d c, d c in next d c, ch 5, join in 3rd st of ch 8.

7th Round—Sl st into loop, ch 3, 3 d c in same space, * d c in next ch 3 loop at top of scallop, ch 2, d c in same space, 4 d c in next loop, ch 1, 4 d c in next loop, ch 1, 4 d c in next loop, repeat from * all around ending to correspond, ch 1, join, cut thread.

8th Round—Ch 5, sl st in any ch 2 loop of 7th round, ch 3, turn, 1 d c in each of the 5 sts of ch just made, ch 3, turn, working in back loop of sts work 1 d c in each of the next 5 sts, ** ch 5, * sl st in next ch 1 space, ch 3, turn, 5 d c over the loop just made, ch 3, turn, working in back loop of sts 1 d c in each of the next 5 sts, ch 5, repeat from * once, sl st in next ch 2 loop, ch 3, turn, 5 d c over loop just made, ch 3, turn, working in back loop of sts 1 d c in each of the next 5 sts (block pattern), repeat from ** all around ending to correspond, join in 1st st of ch.

9th Round—Sl st to point of block pattern, * ch 8, s c in point of next block pattern, repeat from * all around, ch 8, join.

10th Round—Ch 3, * 9 d c in next loop, d c in next s c, repeat from * all around ending with 9 d c in last loop, join in 3rd st of ch.

11th Round—Sl st to 2nd d c, ch 3, 1 d c in each of the next 6 d c, * ch 5, skip 3 d c, 1 d c in each of the next 7 d c, repeat from * all around, ch 5, join.

12th Round—Sl st to next d c, ch 3, 1 d c in each of the next 4 d c, * ch 4, s c in center st of next loop, ch 4, skip 1 d c, 1 d c in each of the next 5 d c, repeat from * all around ending with ch 4, s c in center st of next loop, ch 4, join.

13th Round—Sl st to next d c, ch 3, 1 d c in each of the next 2 d c keeping last loop of each d c on hook, thread over and work off all loops at one time, * ch 6, s c in next s c, ch 6, skip 1 d c, 1 d c in each of the next 3 d c keeping last loop of each d c on hook, thread over and work off all loops at one time, repeat from * all around ending with ch 6, s c in next s c, ch 2, tr c in top of 1st cluster st (this brings thread in position for next round).

14th and 15th Rounds—Ch 10, d c in next loop, * ch 7, d c in next loop, repeat from * all around ending each round with ch 3, tr c in 3rd st of ch.

16th Round—Ch 11, d c in next loop, * ch 8, d c in next loop, repeat from * all around ending with ch 8, sl st in 3rd st of ch.

17th Round—Sl st into loop, ch 3, 6 d c in same loop, * ch 1, 7 d c in next loop, repeat from * all around, ch 1, join in 3rd st of ch, cut thread.

18th Round—Ch 5, sl st in any ch 1 space of last round, * work a block pattern same as 8th round, ch 5, sl st in next ch 1 space, repeat from * all around, join in 1st st of ch.

19th Round—Same as 9th round but having 9 chs in each loop. Repeat the 10th, 11th, 12th, 13th, 14th, 15th and 16th rounds.

27th Round—Start ruffle: sl st into loop, * ch 8, s c in same loop, ch 8, s c in same loop, ch 8, s c in same loop, ch 8, s c in next loop, repeat from * all around ending with ch 4, tr c in sl st (384 loops).

28th Round—* Ch 8, s c in next loop, repeat from * all around ending with ch 4, tr c in tr c. Repeat the 28th round 3 times but ending last round with ch 8, s c in tr c.

32nd Round—Sl st into loop, ch 3, 6 d c in same loop, * ch 4, s c in next loop, ch 4, 7 d c in next loop, repeat from * all around ending with ch 4, s c in next loop, ch 4, join.

33rd Round—Sl st into next st, ch 3, 1 d c in each of the next 4 d c, * ch 6, s c in next s c, ch 6, skip 1 d c, 1 d c in each of the next 5 d c, repeat from * all around ending with ch 6, s c in next s c, ch 6, join.

34th Round—Sl st to next st, ch 3, 1 d c in each of the next 2 d c keeping last loop of each d c on hook, thread over and work off all loops at one time, ch 4, sl st in top of cluster just made for picot, ch 6, s c in next loop, ch 7, s c in next loop, ch 6, skip 1 d c, 1 d c in each of the next 3 d c keeping last loop of each d c on hook, thread over and work off all loops at one time, ch 4, sl st in top of cluster just made for picot, repeat from * all around ending to correspond, join, cut thread.

INSIDE RUFFLE—Attach thread in any loop of 15th round, * ch 8, s c in same loop, ch 8, s c in same loop, ch 8, s c in next loop, repeat from * all around ending with ch 4, tr c in same space as beginning.
Repeat the 28th round twice but ending last round with ch 8, s c in tr c. Repeat the 32nd, 33rd and 34th rounds. ✿

Ruffled Masterpiece

MATERIALS REQUIRED:

DAISY Mercerized Crochet Cotton, Art. 65:—
2 skeins White *and*

1 skein Turquoise, size 30; *or*

DAISY Mercerized Crochet Cotton, Art. 97:—
2 balls each White and Turquoise, size 30; *or*

Lily MERCROCHET Cotton, Art. 161;—

2 balls each White and Turquoise, size 30; *and*

Steel crochet hook No. 13.

SIZE:—With DAISY - 19 inches; with MERCROCHET - 17 inches.

Starting in center:—*COLORED MOTIF*—With Turquoise, ch 8, join with sl st to form ring. *1st rnd*—Ch 1, 12 sc in ring, join with sl st in 1st sc. *2d rnd*—Ch 1, sc in same st, (sc in next 2 sc, ch 6, sc in same sc with last sc) 5 times, sc in next 2 sts, ch 4, join with hdc in 1st sc. *3d rnd*—Ch 3, (in next ch-6 lp make 4 dc, ch 3, 4 dc) 5 times. In final lp make 4 dc, ch 3, 3 dc, join with sl st in top of 1st ch-3. Cut 6 inches long, thread to a needle and fasten off on back.

WHITE MOTIF—With White repeat 1st and 2d rnds. *3d rnd*—Ch 3, (in next ch-6 lp make dc, ch 2, dc, ch 3, dc, ch 2, dc) 5 times. In final lp, make dc, ch 2, dc, ch 1, sl st in a corner ch-3 on Colored Motif, ch 1, dc back in same lp on White Motif, ch 2, join with sl st in top of 1st ch-3. Fasten off in same way, carrying thread down back to center ring to fasten. * Make another White Motif, joining it to the next corner on Colored Motif and to the next free corner on previous White Motif. Repeat from * 3 times. Make a 6th White Motif, joining it to 1st and 5th White Motifs and to remaining corner on Center Motif,—completing row. *3d ROW*—Make a Colored Motif, joining it to 1 corner each on 2 adjoining White Motifs. * Make another Colored Motif, joining it to 1 corner of previous Colored Motif and to the next corner of same White Motif. Make another Colored Motif, joining it to one corner of previous Colored Motif, to the corner of same White Motif and to the next corner of the following White Motif. Repeat from * around, joining 12th Motif to 1st Motif. *4th ROW*—Make 18 White Motifs (1 more on each side than in last row), always starting each row by joining 1st Motif to 1 corner each of 2 adjoining Colored Motifs. *5th ROW*—24 Colored Motifs (1 more on each side than in last row), starting in same way as in last row. *6th ROW*—30 White Motifs. *7th ROW*—36 Colored Motifs.

RUFFLE—Join White to center point on one corner Motif, ch 8, dc in same place, * (ch 10, dc in next point, ch 8, dc in 1st point on next Motif) 6 times, ch 10, (dc, ch 5, dc) in next (corner) point. Repeat from * around, join to 3d st of ch-8. *2d rnd*—Sc in next sp, ** (ch 4, sc in same sp) 3 times, * ch 4, sc in next sp, (ch 4, sc in same sp) 3 times, ch 4, sc in next sp, (ch 4, sc in same sp) twice. Repeat from * across to next corner sp. Repeat from ** around, ch 4, join to 1st sc. *3d rnd*—Sl st to center of next lp, ch 4, hdc in next (corner) lp, * ch 3, hdc in same lp, (ch 2, hdc in next lp) repeated to center lp at next corner. Repeat from * around, ch 2, join to 2d st of ch-4. *4th rnd*—3 sc in next sp, * 5 sc in next (corner) ch-3 sp, (3 sc in next sp) repeated to last sp before corner sp. Repeat from * around. Sl st in 1st 2 sc. *5th rnd*—Ch 5, dc in next sc, (ch 2, dc in next sc) 3 times to center sc at corner, * ch 2, dc in same corner sc, (ch 2, dc in next sc) 4 times, (ch 2, sk 2 sc, dc in next sc) repeated across to last sp before corner sp, (ch 2, dc in next sc) 4 times to center sc at corner. Repeat from * around, ch 2, join to 3d st of ch-5. *6th rnd*—Sc in next sp, ch 3, (dc, ch 3, 2 dc) in same sp, * (ch 5, dc in next sp) 3 times, ch 5, in next sp make a 2 dc, ch 3, 2 dc shell. Repeat from * around, ch 5, join to top of ch-3, sl st to center sp of same shell. *7th rnd*—Ch 5, (2 tr, ch 3, 3 tr) in same place, * (ch 6, dc in next sp) 4 times, ch 6, in next shell make a 3 tr, ch 3, 3 tr shell. Repeat from * around, join to top of ch-5, sl st to center of same shell. *8th rnd*—Repeat last row to *. * (Ch 7, dc in next sp) 5 times, ch 7, a 3 tr, ch 3, 3 tr shell in next shell. Repeat from * around, join, sl st to center of same shell. *9th rnd*—Ch 5, (3 tr, ch 5, 4 tr) in same place, * (ch 8, dc in next sp) 6 times, ch 8, a 4 tr, ch 5, 4 tr shell in next shell. Repeat from * around, join, sl st to center of same shell. *10th rnd*—Repeat last row but with 8 ch-9 lps between shells. *11th rnd*—Ch 5, (4 tr, ch 6, 5 tr) in same shell, * (ch 10, dc in next sp) 8 times, ch 10, a 5 tr, ch 6, 5 tr shell in next shell. Repeat from * around, join and fasten off.

Edge—Join Turquoise to 1st tr on one shell, ch 1, sc in same tr, sc in next 4 tr, 4 sc in half of next sp, ch 5, sl st in last sc for a p, 3 sc in bal. of sp, sc in next 5 tr, (6 sc, a p, 5 sc) in each of next 8 sps, 6 sc in half of next sp, ch 2, sl st back in 8th p from hook, ch 2, sl st back in last sc, 5 sc in bal. of sp, * sc in next 5 tr, (4 sc, a p, 3 sc) in center of shell, sc in next 5 tr, (6 sc, a p, 5 sc) in each of next 2 sps, 6 sc in half of next sp, ch 2, sk last joining of ps, sl st back in 2d previous p, ch 2, sl st back in last sc, 5 sc in same sp, (6 sc, a p, 5 sc) in each of next 5 sps, 6 sc in half of next sp, ch 2, sl st back in 1st p to left of last shell, ch 2, sl st back in last sc, 5 sc in bal. of same sp. Repeat from * around. Fasten off. Tack 1st and last ripples tog. in pattern. Starch doily. When partially dry, stretch and pin it right-side-up in true shape, putting a pin in each shell point around ruffle. Crush a small piece of tissue paper and tuck in each top ripple of ruffle. Let stand until dry. ✤

Sunshine

Materials Required: AMERICAN THREAD COMPANY "GEM" MERCERIZED CROCHET COTTON, Article 35, size 30

3 balls White, Dk. Cream or Ecru or

"STAR" MERCERIZED CROCHET COTTON, Article 20, size 30

4 balls White, Dk. Cream or Ecru
Steel crochet hook No. 12

Doily measures approximately 12½ inches in diameter without ruffle.

Chain (ch) 10, join to form a ring, ch 4, double crochet (d c) in ring, * ch 1, d c in ring, repeat from * 11 times, ch 1, join in 3rd stitch (st) of ch (14 d c).

2nd Round. Ch 3, d c in same space, * ch 2, 2 d c in next d c, repeat from * all around, ch 2, join in 3rd st of ch.

3rd Round. Ch 3, d c in next d c, 1 d c in next st of ch, * ch 2, 1 d c in each of the next 2 d c, 1 d c in next st of ch, repeat from * all around, ch 2, join.

4th Round. Ch 3, 1 d c in each of the next 2 d c, d c in next st of ch, * ch 2, 1 d c in each of the next 3 d c, d c in next st of ch, repeat from * all around, ch 2, join. Repeat the 4th round having 1 more d c in each d c section until there are 8 d c in each section.

9th Round. Ch 3, 1 d c in each of the next 6 d c, * pull up ⅛ inch loop on hook, thread over and pull through loop, single crochet (s c) in single loop of st (single knot st), pull up ⅛ inch loop on hook, thread over and pull through loop, s c in single loop of st (double knot st), 1 d c in each of the next 7 d c of next d c group, repeat from * all around ending with double knot st, join.

10th Round. Ch 3, 1 d c in each of the next 5 d c, * ch 4, s c in center of next double knot st, ch 4, 1 d c in each of the next 6 d c, repeat from * all around ending with ch 4, s c in center of next double knot st, ch 4, join.

11th Round. Ch 3, 1 d c in each of the next 4 d c, * ch 5, s c in next s c, ch 5, 1 d c in each of the next 5 d c, repeat from * all around ending to correspond, ch 5, join.

12th Round. Ch 3, 1 d c in each of the next 3 d c, * ch 5, s c in next loop, double knot st, s c in next loop, ch 5, 1 d c in each of the next 4 d c, repeat from * all around ending to correspond, ch 5, join.

13th Round. Ch 3, 1 d c in each of the next 2 d c, * ch 5, s c in next loop, ch 5, s c in center of next double knot st, ch 5, s c in next loop, ch 5, 1 d c in each of the next 3 d c, repeat from * all around ending to correspond, ch 5, join.

14th Round. Ch 3, d c in next d c, ** ch 4, s c in next loop, * double knot st, s c in next loop, repeat from * twice, ch 4, 1 d c in each of the next 2 d c, repeat from ** all around ending to correspond, ch 4, join.

15th Round. Ch 5, skip next ch 4 loop, s c in center of next double knot st, * ch 5, s c in center of next double knot st, repeat from * once, ch 5, skip 1 loop, s c in next d c, repeat from beginning all around ending with ch 2, d c in same space as beginning (this brings thread in position for next round).

16th Round. * Double knot st, s c in next loop, repeat from * all around ending with double knot st, join in d c.

17th Round. Slip stitch (sl st) to center of next double knot st, * ch 6, s c in center of next double knot st, repeat from * all around ending with ch 3, d c in last sl st.

18th Round. Ch 9, d c in next loop, * ch 6, d c in next loop, repeat from * all around, ch 6, join in 3rd st of ch.

19th Round. Ch 9, d c in next d c, * ch 6, d c in next d c, repeat from * all around, ch 6, join in 3rd st of ch.

20th Round. Sl st to center of next loop, * ch 7, s c in next loop, repeat from * all around ending with ch 3, treble crochet (tr c) in last sl st.

21st Round. Ch 10, d c in next loop, * ch 7, d c in next loop, repeat from * all around, ending with ch 7, join in 3rd st of ch.

22nd Round. Sl st into loop, ch 3, 5 d c in same loop, * ch 5, s c in next loop, ch 5, 6 d c in next loop, repeat from * all around ending with ch 5, s c in next loop, ch 5, join.

23rd Round. Sl st to next d c, ch 3, 1 d c in each of the next 4 d c, * ch 6, s c in next s c, ch 6, skip 1 d c, 1 d c in each of the next 5 d c, repeat from * all around ending to correspond, ch 6, join.

24th Round. Sl st to next d c, ch 3, 1 d c in each of the next 3 d c, * ch 7, 1 d c in each of the next 2 loops keeping last loop of each d c on hook, thread over and work off all loops at one time (d c joining), ch 7, skip 1 d c, 1 d c in each of the next 4 d c, repeat from * all around ending to correspond, ch 7, join.

25th Round. Sl st to next d c, ch 3, 1 d c in each of the next 2 d c, * ch 4, s c in next loop, ch 4, d c in next d c joining, ch 4, s c in next loop, ch 4, skip 1 d c, 1 d c in each of the next 3 d c, repeat from * all around ending to correspond, ch 4, join.

26th Round. Sl st to next d c, ch 3, d c in next d c, * ch 7, skip 1 loop, s c over end of next loop, s c in next d c, s c over beginning of next loop, ch 7, skip 1 loop and 1 d c, 1 d c in each of the next 2 d c, repeat from * all around ending to correspond, ch 7, join.

27th Round. Ch 8, s c in next loop, * ch 5, d c in center s c of next s c group, ch 5, s c in next loop, ch 5, skip 1 d c, d c in next d c, ch 5, s c in next loop, repeat from * all around in same manner, ending with ch 2, d c in 3rd st of ch.

28th and 29th Rounds. * Ch 6, s c in next loop, repeat from * all around ending each round with ch 3, d c in d c.

30th Round. Same as last round but ending with ch 1, double treble crochet [d tr c (3 times over hook)] in d c.

31st Round. Ch 3, 5 d c over d tr c just made, * ch 3, s c in next loop, ch 5, d c in next loop, ch 5, s c in next loop, ch 3, 6 d c in next loop, repeat from * all around ending to correspond.

32nd Round. Sl st to next d c, ch 3, 1 d c in each of the next 4 d c, * ch 8, skip 1 loop, s c over end of next loop, s c in next d c, s c over beginning of next loop, ch 8, skip 1 loop and 1 d c, 1 d c in each of the next 5 d c, repeat from * all around ending to correspond, ch 8, join.

33rd Round. Sl st to next d c, ch 3, 1 d c in each of the next 3 d c, * ch 5, s c in next loop, ch 5, d c in center s c of next s c group, ch 5, s c in next loop, ch 5, skip 1 d c, 1 d c in each of the next 4 d c, repeat from * all around ending to correspond, ch 5, join.

34th Round. Sl st to next d c, ch 3, 1 d c in each of the next 2 d c, * ch 6, d c in next s c, ch 6, s c in next d c, ch 6, d c in next s c, ch 6, skip 1 d c, 1 d c in each of the next 3 d c, repeat from * all around ending to correspond, ch 6, join.

35th Round. Sl st to next d c, ch 3, d c in next d c, * ch 6, s c in next d c, ch 6, 1 d c in each of the next 2 loops keeping last loop of each d c on hook, thread over and work off all loops at one time, ch 6, s c in next d c, ch 6, skip 1 d c, 1 d c in each of the next 2 d c, repeat from * all around ending to correspond, ch 6, join.

36th Round. Sl st to next d c, ch 10, s c in next s c, * ch 7, d c in next d c joining, ch 7, s c in next s c, ch 7, skip 1 d c, d c in next d c, ch 7, s c in next s c, repeat from * all around ending to correspond, ch 3, tr c in 3rd st of ch.

37th Round. * Ch 7, s c in next loop, repeat from * all around ending with ch 3, tr c in tr c.

38th Round. Same as last round but ending with ch 7, s c in tr c.

Next Round. Start outside ruffle: sl st into loop, * ch 8, s c in same loop, ch 8, s c in same loop, ch 8, s c in next loop, ch 8, s c in same loop, ch 8, s c in same loop, ch 8, s c in same loop, ch 8, s c in next loop, repeat from * all around ending with ch 4, tr c in sl st (392 loops).

2nd and 3rd Rounds. * Ch 8, s c in next loop, repeat from * all around ending each round with ch 4, tr c in tr c.

4th Round. * Work a double knot st pulling loop up ¼ inch, s c in next loop, repeat from * all around.

5th, 6th and 7th Rounds. Sl st to center of next double knot st, * work a double knot st, s c in center s c of next double knot st, repeat from * all around.

8th Round. Sl st to center of double knot st, * ch 8, s c in center s c of next double knot st, repeat from * all around ending with ch 4, d tr c in sl st.

9th Round. ** Ch 5, tr c in next loop, * ch 4, sl st in 4th st from hook for picot, tr c in same loop, repeat from * 3 times, ch 5, s c in next loop, repeat from ** all around, join, cut thread.

Inside Ruffle: Attach thread in any mesh of 18th round and work same as outside ruffle having 196 loops in 1st round but working only 2 rounds of 8 ch loops and 3 rounds of double knot sts. Work last 2 rounds same as last 2 rounds of outside ruffle.❁

Star Spangled Ruffled Doily

Materials Required: AMERICAN THREAD COMPANY The Famous "PURITAN" STAR SPANGLED CROCHET COTTON, Article 40.

5 balls Yellow Spangle or color of your choice for large doily.

2 balls for small doily, or

The Famous "PURITAN" CROCHET COTTON, Article 40.

3 balls Yellow or color of your choice for large doily.

1 ball for small doily.

Large doily measures 12 inches in diameter without the ruffle.

Small doily measures 7 inches in diameter without ruffle.

Steel crochet hook No. 7.

LARGE DOILY
Shown in color on the inside front cover.

Ch 2, 8 s c in 2nd st from hook, join in 1st s c.

2nd Round. Ch 1 and work 2 s c in each s c, join in 1st s c (16 s c).

3rd Round. * 1 s c in next s c, 2 s c in next s c, repeat from * all around (24 s c), join.

4th Round. 1 s c in each s c, join.

5th Round. * Ch 5, skip 1 s c, s c in next s c, repeat from * 10 times, ch 2, d c in same space as beginning (this brings thread in position for next round).

6th Round. * Ch 5, s c in next loop, repeat from * all around ending with ch 5, s c in d c.

7th Round. Sl st into loop, ch 3, 1 d c, ch 5, 2 d c in same loop, * 2 d c, ch 5, 2 d c in next loop, repeat from * all around, join in 3rd st of ch.

8th Round. Sl st into loop, ch 3, 1 d c, ch 3, 2 d c in same loop, * ch 3, 2 d c, ch 3, 2 d c (shell) in next loop, repeat from * all around, ch 3, join in 3rd st of ch.

9th Round. Sl st into loop, ch 3, 1 d c, ch 3, 2 d c in same space, * ch 5, shell in center of next shell, repeat from * all around, ch 5, join.

10th Round. Sl st to center of shell, ch 3, 1 d c, ch 3, 2 d c in same space, * ch 4, s c over the 2 loops of 2 previous rounds, ch 4, shell in next shell, repeat from * all around ending to correspond, join each round.

11th Round. Sl st to center of shell, ch 3, 1 d c, ch 3, 2 d c in same space, * ch 4, tr c in next s c, ch 4, shell in next shell, repeat from * all around ending to correspond.

12th Round. Sl st to center of shell, ch 3, 1 d c, ch 3, 2 d c in same space, * ch 4, s c in next loop, s c in next tr c, s c in next loop, ch 4, shell in next shell, repeat from * all around ending to correspond.

13th Round. Sl st to center of shell, ch 3, 1 d c, ch 3, 2 d c in same space, * ch 5, 1 s c in each of the next 3 s c, ch 5, shell in next shell, repeat from * all around ending to correspond.

14th Round. Sl st to center of shell, ch 3, 1 d c, ch 3, 2 d c in same space, * ch 6, thread over hook twice, insert in next loop, pull through and work off 2 loops twice, thread over hook twice, insert in next loop, pull through and work off 2 loops twice, thread over and work off all loops at one time (tr c cluster), ch 6, shell in next shell, repeat from * all around ending to correspond.

15th Round. Sl st to center of shell, ch 3, 1 d c, ch 3, 2 d c in same space, * ch 5, shell in next tr c cluster, ch 5, shell in next shell, repeat from * all around ending to correspond.

16th Round. Sl st to center of shell, ch 3, 1 d c, ch 3, 2 d c in same space, * ch 4, s c over the 2 loops of 2 previous rounds, ch 4, shell in next shell, repeat from * all around ending to correspond.

17th Round. Sl st to center of shell, ch 3, 1 d c, ch 3, 2 d c in same space, * ch 3, tr c in next s c, ch 3, shell in next shell, repeat from * all around ending to correspond.

18th and 19th Rounds. Same as 12th and 13th rounds.

20th Round. Same as 14th round but having ch 5 before and after each tr c cluster.

21st Round. Sl st into shell, * ch 6, s c in next loop, ch 6, s c in next loop, ch 6, s c in center of next shell, repeat from * all around.

22nd Round. Start Ruffle: Sl st into loop, * ch 6, s c in same loop, ch 6, s c in same loop, ch 6, s c in same loop, ch 6, s c in next loop, repeat from * all around.

23rd Round. Sl st to center of loop, * ch 6, s c in next loop, repeat from * all around ending with ch 3, d c in sl st, this brings thread in position for next round.

24th and 25th Rounds. * Ch 6, s c in next loop, repeat from * all around ending each round with ch 3, d c in d c.

26th Round. * Ch 3, 2 d c, ch 3, 2 d c in next loop, ch 3, s c in next loop, repeat from * all around.

27th Round. * Ch 4, shell in next shell, ch 4, s c in next s c, repeat from * all around.

28th Round. Sl st into loop, * ch 3, 2 d c in center of next shell, ch 4, sl st in 3rd st from hook for picot, ch 1, 2 d c in same space, ch 3, s c in next loop, ch 4, sl st in 3rd st from hook for picot, ch 1, s c in next loop, repeat from * all around ending to correspond, join, cut thread. ✼

SMALL DOILY *Shown in the photograph below.*
Work 1st 14 rounds same as large doily.

15th, 16th and 17 rounds. Same as 21st, 22nd and 23rd rounds of large doily.

18th, 19th and 20th Rounds. Same as 26th, 27th and 28th rounds of large doily. ✼

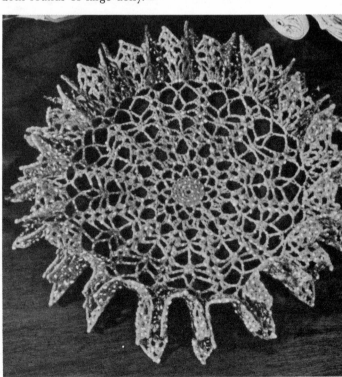

Shooting Star

Materials Required:

MERCERIZED CROCHET COTTON, Size 30

4—100 yd. Balls White.

Steel Crochet Hook No. 12.

Doily measures about 7 inches without ruffle.

Ch 8, join to form a ring and work 16 s c in ring, join.

2nd Row. Ch 8, tr c in same space, * skip 1 s c, 2 tr c with ch 4 between in next s c, repeat from * 6 times, join in 4th st of ch.

3rd Row. 3 s c, ch 5, 3 s c over each ch 4 loop, join.

4th Row. Sl st to center of 5 ch loop, s c in same space, * ch 5, skip 2 s c, tr c in space between next 2 s c, ch 5, s c in next 5 ch loop, repeat from * 6 times, ch 5, skip 2 s c, tr c in space between next 2 s c, ch 2, tr c in 1st s c, this brings thread in position for next row.

5th Row. S c in same space, * ch 7, 5 tr c (shell) in next tr c, ch 7, skip 1 loop, s c in next loop, 7 tr c in next tr c, s c in next loop, repeat from * all around in same manner ending row with sl st in 1st s c.

6th Row. Sl st to center of loop, s c in same space, * ch 9, s c in center tr c of next shell, ch 9, s c in next loop, ch 11, s c in center tr c of next tr c group, ch 11, s c in next loop, repeat from * all around in same manner ending row with ch 6, d tr c (3 times over needle) in 1st s c.

7th Row. Ch 11, s c in next loop, repeat from beginning all around ending row with ch 6, tr tr c (4 times over needle) in d tr c.

8th Row. Ch 4, 4 tr c in same space, * ch 9, s c in next loop, ch 9, 2 shells with ch 5 between in center st of next loop, repeat from * 6 times, ch 9, s c in next loop, ch 9, 5 tr c in same space as 1st shell, ch 2, d c in 4th st of ch.

9th Row. Ch 5, shell in center st of next shell, ch 3, s c in next loop, ch 9, s c in next loop, ch 3, shell in center st of next shell, ch 5, s c in next loop, repeat from beginning all around in same manner ending row with ch 2, d c in d c.

10th Row. Ch 5, s c in next loop, ch 5, shell in center st of next shell, ch 5, skip 1 loop, s c in next loop, ch 5, shell in center st of next shell, ch 5, s c in next loop, repeat from beginning all around in same manner ending row with ch 2, d c in d c.

11th Row. Ch 5, s c in next loop, ch 5, s c in next loop, ch 5, shell in center st of next shell, ch 3, shell in center st of next shell, ch 5, s c in next loop, repeat from beginning all around in same manner ending row with ch 2, d c in d c.

12th Row. * Ch 5, s c in next loop, repeat from * twice, ch 5, * shell in center st of next shell, repeat from *, repeat from beginning all around in same manner ending row with ch 2, d c in d c.

13th Row. * Ch 7, s c in next loop, repeat from * 3 times, ch 7, * thread over twice, insert in next tr c, pull through, thread over and work off 2 loops twice, repeat from * 9 times, thread over and work off all loops at one time (cluster st) ch 7, s c in next loop, repeat from beginning all around in same manner ending row with ch 3, tr c in d c.

14th Row. * Ch 7, s c in next loop, repeat from * 4 times, ch 7, s c in top of next cluster st, ch 7, s c in next loop, repeat from * all around in same manner ending row with ch 3, tr c in tr c.

15th and 16th Rows. * Ch 8, s c in next loop, repeat from * all around ending row with ch 4, tr c in tr c.

17th Row. Shell in same space as tr c just made, s c in next loop, * ch 7, s c in next loop, shell in next s c, s c in next loop, repeat from * in same manner all around ending row with ch 3, tr c in tr c.

continued on page 36

Zephyr

MATERIALS: J. & P. Coats or Clark's O.N.T. Best Six Cord Mercerized Crochet, *Size 30:* **Small Ball:** J. & P. Coats—*3 balls of White or Ecru, or 4 balls of any color, or* Clark's O.N.T.—*5 balls of White or Ecru, or 7 balls of any color* . . . Steel Crochet Hook No. 10.

Doily measures 18 inches in diameter

Starting at center, ch 12. Join with sl st to form ring. **1st rnd:** Ch 3, 23 dc in ring. Join to top of ch-3. **2nd rnd:** Sc in same place as sl st, sc in each dc around. Join. **3rd rnd:** Ch 6, tr tr in same place as sl st, * ch 5, skip next sc, 2 tr tr in next sc. Repeat from * around. Join. **4th rnd:** Sc between starting chain and next tr tr, * in next sp make half dc, 2 dc, 3 tr, 2 dc and half dc (petal); sc between next 2 tr tr. Repeat from * around. Join. **5th rnd:** Sl st in next 2 sts, ch 11, * skip 4 sts, tr tr in next st, ch 5, skip 2 sts on next petal, tr tr in next st, ch 5. Repeat from * around. Join to 6th ch of ch-11. **6th rnd:** Sc in same place as sl st, * ch 9, sc in next tr tr. Repeat from * around, ending with ch 4, d tr in first sc. **7th rnd:** * Ch 10, sc in next loop. Repeat from * around, ending with ch 5, d tr in d tr. **8th rnd:** Ch 9, * holding back on hook the last loop of each tr tr make 4 tr tr in 6th ch from hook, thread over and draw through all loops on hook (cluster made), in 5th ch of next loop make 5-tr tr cluster, ch 6; make 4-tr tr cluster in 6th ch from hook, dc in next loop, ch 9, sc in next loop, ch 9, dc in next loop, ch 6. Repeat from * around. Join last ch-9 to 3rd st of starting chain. **9th rnd:** Ch 8, cluster in tip of center cluster of next 3-cluster group, * (ch 8, cluster in same place) twice; long tr (thread over hook 5 times) in next dc, (ch 6, tr tr in next loop) twice; ch 6, long tr in next dc, cluster in tip of center cluster of next cluster-group. Repeat from * around, ending with ch 4, tr in tip of first cluster. **10th rnd:** Ch 13, dc in next loop, (ch 10, dc in next loop) twice; * ch 6, sc in next loop, ch 6, dc in next loop, (ch 10, dc in next loop) 3 times. Repeat from * around, ending with ch 4, half dc in 3rd st of ch-13. **11th rnd:** Ch 3, sc in same ch as half dc, (ch 3, skip 1 st, sc in next st) 17 times; * ch 8, skip next sc and next 4 ch, sc in next ch, (ch 3, skip next st, sc in next st) 18 times. Repeat from * around. Join.

12th rnd: Sl st to center of next loop, * (ch 3, sc in next loop) 17 times; (ch 6, sc in next loop) twice. Repeat from * around. Join. **13th rnd:** Sl st to center st of second loop, sc in loop, * (ch 3, sc in next loop) 14 times; ch 6, skip next ch-3 loop, sc in next loop, ch 6, sc in next loop, ch 6, skip next ch-3 loop, sc in next loop. Repeat from * around, ending with ch 3, dc in first sc. **14th rnd:** * Ch 6, skip next ch-3 loop, sc in next loop, (ch 3, sc in next loop) 11 times; (ch 6, sc in next ch-6 loop) 3 times. Repeat from * around, ending with ch 3, dc in dc. **15th rnd:** Ch 6, sc in next loop, * ch 6, skip next ch-3 loop, sc in next loop, (ch 3, sc in next loop) 8 times; (ch 6, sc in next ch-6 loop) 4 times. Repeat from * around. Join as before. **16th rnd:** (Ch 7, sc in next loop) twice; * ch 7, skip next ch-3 loop, sc in next loop, (ch 3, sc in next loop) 5 times; (ch 7, sc in next ch-6 loop) 5 times. Repeat from * around, ending with ch 3, tr in dc. **17th rnd:** (Ch 7, sc in next loop) 3 times; * ch 7, skip 1 loop, sc in next loop, ch 5, skip next loop, sc in next loop, (ch 7, sc in next ch-7 loop) 6 times. Repeat from * around, ending with ch 3, tr in tr. **18th rnd:** Ch 11, tr in next loop, * ch 7, tr in next loop. Repeat from * around. Join last ch 7 to 4th st of ch-11. **19th rnd:** 9 sc in each sp around. Join.

RUFFLE . . . 1st rnd: Ch 10, * skip 1 sc, tr in next sc, ch 6. Repeat from * around, ending with ch 3, dc in 4th ch of ch-10. **2nd and 3rd rnds:** Ch 10, * tr in next sp, ch 6. Repeat from * around, ending with ch 3, dc in 4th ch of ch-10. **4th, 5th and 6th rnds:** Ch 11, * tr in next sp, ch 7. Repeat from * around, ending with ch 3, tr in 4th ch of ch-11. **7th, 8th and 9th rnds:** Ch 12, * tr in next sp, ch 8. Repeat from * around, ending with ch 4, tr in 4th ch of ch-12. **10th to 14th rnds incl:** Ch 13, * tr in next sp, ch 9. Repeat from * around, ending with ch 4, d tr in 4th ch of ch-13. Join and break off. Starch lightly and press. ✳

Stardust

MATERIALS: J. & P. Coats or Clark's O.N.T. Best Six Cord Mercerized Crochet, *Size 30:* **Small Ball:** J. & P. Coats—*2 balls of White or Ecru,* or *3 balls of any color,* or Clark's O.N.T.—*3 balls of White or Ecru, or 4 balls of any color.* **Big Ball:** J. & P. Coats—*1 ball of White, Ecru or Cream . . . Steel Crochet Hook No. 10 or 11.*

Starting at center, ch 10. Join with sl st to form ring. **1st rnd:** Ch 3, 23 dc in ring. Sl st in top st of ch-3. **2nd rnd:** Ch 8, * skip 1 dc, dc in next dc, ch 5. Repeat from * around, ending with ch 5, sl st in 3rd st of ch-8. **3rd rnd:** Sl st in next 2 sts, sc in sp, ch 8, * dc in next sp, ch 5. Repeat from * around. Join as before. **4th rnd:** Ch 3, * 7 dc in sp, dc in dc. Repeat from * around. Sl st in 3rd st of ch-3. **5th rnd:** Sl st in next dc, ch 3, dc in next 14 dc, * ch 5, skip 1 dc, dc in next 15 dc. Repeat from * around. Join last ch-5 with sl st to top of ch-3. **6th rnd:** Sl st in next dc, ch 3, * dc in each dc to within last dc of this group, ch 5, sc in next loop, ch 5, skip next dc. Repeat from * around. Join. **7th rnd:** Sl st in next dc, ch 3, * dc in each dc to within last dc of this group, (ch 5, sc in next loop) twice; ch 5, skip next dc. Repeat from * around. Join. **8th to 11th rnds incl:** Work as for previous rnd, having 1 more loop between dc-groups on each rnd. **12th rnd:** Sl st in next dc, ch 8, * sc in next loop, (ch 5, sc in next loop) 6 times; ch 5, skip 1 dc, dc in next dc, ch 5. Repeat from * around. Join. **13th rnd:** Sl st in next 3 ch, ch 8, * dc in next loop, ch 5. Repeat from * around. Join. **14th rnd:** Ch 3, * 5 dc in sp, dc in next dc. Repeat from * around. Join. **15th rnd:** Sc in same place as sl st, * ch 7, skip 1 dc, sc in next dc. Repeat from * around, ending with ch 3, tr in first sc. **16th to 19th rnds incl:** * Ch 7, sc in next loop. Repeat from * around, ending with ch 3, tr in tr. **20th rnd:** Same as 19th rnd, making ch-8 (instead of ch-7) loops and ending with ch 4, tr in tr. **21st rnd:** Same as previous rnd, making ch-9 loops and ending with ch 4, d tr in tr. **22nd rnd:** Make ch-10 loops around, ending with ch 5, d tr in d tr. **23rd rnd:** Make ch-11 loops around, ending with ch 11, sl st in d tr. Break off. ✳

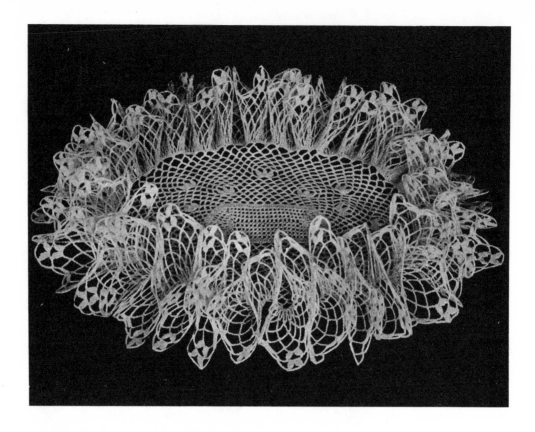

Edelweiss

Materials Required— MERCERIZED CROCHET COTTON, Size 30 or 50

3—150 Yd. Balls White or any Color Desired.
Steel Crochet Hook No. 11 or 12.
Doily measures about 9 x 12 inches.

Ch 35 and work 6 d c with ch 1 between each d c in 5th st from hook, * ch 1, skip 1 ch, 1 d c in next ch, repeat from * 13 times, ch 1 and work 7 d c with ch 1 between each d c in last st of ch, working on other side of ch, work other side to correspond, join each row.

2nd Row. Ch 4, work 3 d c with ch 1 between each d c in next d c, work 1 d c with ch 1 between in each of next 3 d c, work 3 d c with ch 1 between each d c in next d c, work 1 d c with ch 1 between each of next 16 d c, then work other side to correspond.

3rd Row. Ch 4, d c in next d c, ch 1, 3 d c with ch 1 between each d c in next d c, * work 1 d c with ch 1 between in each of next 2 d c, 3 d c with ch 1 between in next d c, repeat from *, then work 1 d c with ch 1 between in each of next 17 d c and finish other side to correspond.

4th Row. Same as 3rd row, working 3 d c with ch 1 between in center d c of each increasing point (6 increasing points in row).

5th Row. Work 1 d c in each mesh and d c working 3 d c in center d c of each increasing point.

6th Row. * Ch 5, skip 3 d c, s c in next d c, repeat from * all around, always sl st to center of loop.

7th, 8th and 9th Rows. * Ch 5, s c in next loop, repeat from * all around.

10th Row. Ch 5, s c in next loop, ch 5, ** work 3 cluster sts with ch 5 between each cluster st in next loop, (cluster st: * thread over needle twice, insert in loop, draw through, work off 2 loops twice, repeat from * twice, then work off all loops 2 at a time). * Ch 5, s c in next loop, repeat from * twice, ch 5, repeat from **, ch 5, work 3 cluster sts with ch 5 between in next loop, ch 5, s c in next loop, work a 5 ch loop in each of next 6 loops, ch 5, work 3 cluster sts with ch 5 between in next loop, * ch 5, s c in next loop, repeat from * twice, ch 5, then work other side to correspond.

11th, 12th, 13th and 14th Rows. Work a 5 ch loop in each loop.

15th Row. Ch 5, s c in next loop, ch 5, s c in next loop, ch 5, work 3 cluster sts with ch 5 between in next loop, * ch 5, s c in next loop, repeat from * 4 times, ** ch 5, work 3 cluster sts with ch 5 between in next loop, * ch 5, s c in next loop, repeat from * 6 times, then repeat from **, ch 5, work 3 cluster sts with ch 5 between in next loop, * ch 5, s c in next loop, repeat from * 4 times, then work other side to correspond.

16th, 17th, 18th and 19th Rows. Repeat 11th, 12th, 13th and 14th rows.

20th and 21st Rows. Work a 6 ch loop in each loop.

22nd Row. * Work 6 s c in next loop, 5 s c in next loop, repeat from * all around.

23rd Row. * Ch 10, s c in next s c, repeat from * all around. (Do not join this or following rows). Work 4 more rows of 10 ch loops.

Edge. * Ch 6, cluster st in next loop, ch 5, cluster st in same loop, ch 6, work 6 s c in each of next 2 loops, repeat from * all around, join.

Next Row. Sl st to center of next loop, * ch 7, work 2 cluster sts with ch 7 between in next loop, ch 7, s c in next loop, ch 7, s c in center of s c group, ch 7, s c in next loop, repeat from * all around. ✿

Rolling Ruffles

Make this doily with any of the
AMERICAN THREAD COMPANY products listed below:

Material	Quantity	Approx. Size of Doily without Ruffle	Size of Needle
"GEM" CROCHET COTTON Article 35, size 30	2 balls White	9½ inches x 12¾ inches	steel 11 or 12
or "PURITAN" CROCHET COTTON Article 40	2 balls White	13½ inches x 16 inches	steel 7
or "DE LUXE" CROCHET COTTON Article 346	2 balls White	13½ inches x 16 inches	steel 7

Ch 72, s c in 12th st from hook, * ch 5, skip 5 sts of ch, s c in next st, repeat from * 8 times, ch 5, join in end st of ch.

2nd Round—Ch 1, s c in loop, ch 3, 3 s c, ch 3, 3 s c in same loop, * 7 s c in next loop, 3 s c, ch 3, 3 s c in next loop, repeat from * 3 times, 7 s c in next loop, 3 s c, ch 3, 3 s c, ch 3, 3 s c in next loop, * 7 s c in next loop, 3 s c, ch 3, 3 s c in next loop, repeat from * 3 times, 7 s c in next loop, 3 s c, ch 3, 2 s c in end loop.

3rd Round—Sl st to loop, ch 4, 2 tr c, ch 3, 3 tr c in same loop, * ch 3, 3 tr c, ch 3, 3 tr c (shell) in next loop, ch 3, skip 6 s c, s c in next s c, repeat from * 4 times, ch 3, shell in next loop, ch 3, shell in next loop, ch 3, shell in next loop, * ch 3, skip 6 s c, s c in next s c, ch 3, shell in next loop, repeat from * 4 times, ch 3, join in 4th st of ch.

4th Round—Sl st to loop, ch 3, 2 d c in same space keeping last loop of each st on hook, thread over and pull through all loops at one time, ch 11, 1 d c, ch 3, 1 d c in next loop, ch 9, cluster st in loop of next shell (cluster st: 3 d c in loop keeping last loop of each st on hook, thread over and work off all loops at one time), ch 9, s c in next loop, ch 3, s c in next loop, * ch 7, cluster st in next shell, ch 7, s c in next loop, ch 3, s c in next loop, repeat from * 3 times, ch 7, cluster st in next shell, ch 9, 1 d c, ch 3, 1 d c in next loop, ch 11, cluster st in next shell, ch 11, 1 d c, ch 3, 1 d c in next loop, ch 9, cluster st in next shell, ch 9, s c in next loop, ch 3, s c in next loop, * ch 7, cluster st in next shell, ch 7, s c in next loop, ch 3, s c in next loop, repeat from * 3 times, ch 9, cluster st in next shell, ch 9, 1 d c, ch 3, 1 d c in next loop, ch 5, tr tr c in 1st cluster st (this brings thread in position for next round).

5th Round—** Ch 13, s c in next loop, ch 13, skip the ch 3 loop, s c in next loop, ch 5, s c in next loop, * ch 9, skip the ch 3 loop, s c in next loop, ch 5, s c in next loop, repeat from * 4 times, ch 13, skip the ch 3 loop, s c in next loop, repeat from ** all around ending to correspond, join in tr tr c.

continued overleaf

6th Round—Sl st to 4th st of ch, ch 3 (always counts as part of 1st cluster st), cluster st in same space, ch 5, cluster st in same loop, ch 5, cluster st in same loop, ch 5, s c in next s c, ch 5, 3 cluster sts with ch 5 between each cluster st in next loop, ch 5, s c in next loop, * ch 5, 2 cluster sts with ch 5 between in next loop, ch 5, s c in next loop, repeat from * 4 times, * ch 5, 3 cluster sts with ch 5 between each cluster st in next loop, ch 5, s c in next s c, repeat from * once, ch 5, 3 cluster sts with ch 5 between each cluster st in next loop, ch 5, s c in next loop, finish side and end to correspond, join in 1st cluster st.

7th Round—Sl st to loop, ch 3, cluster st in same space, ** ch 7, cluster st in next loop, ch 7, s c in next loop, ch 3, s c in next loop, ch 7, cluster st in next loop, ch 7, cluster st in next loop, ch 7, s c in next loop, ch 3, s c in next loop, ch 7, cluster st in loop between next 2 cluster sts, ch 7, s c in next loop, ch 3, s c in next loop, repeat from * 4 times, ch 7, cluster st in next loop, ch 7, cluster st in next loop, ch 7, s c in next loop, ch 3, s c in next loop, ch 7, cluster st in next loop, repeat from ** all around omitting last cluster st, join in 1st cluster st.

8th Round—Sl st into loop, ch 3, cluster st in same space, ch 9, s c in next loop, ch 11, skip 1 loop, s c in next loop, ch 9, cluster st in next loop, ch 9, s c in next loop, * ch 9, skip 1 loop, s c in next loop, ch 7, s c in next loop, repeat from * 4 times, ch 9, skip 1 loop, s c in next loop, * ch 9, cluster st in next loop, ch 9, s c in next loop, ch 11, skip 1 loop, s c in next loop, repeat from * once, ch 9, cluster st in next loop, ch 9, s c in next loop, * ch 9, skip 1 loop, s c in next loop, ch 7, s c in next loop, repeat from * 4 times, ch 9, skip 1 loop, s c in next loop, ch 9, cluster st in next loop, ch 9, s c in next loop, ch 11, skip 1 loop, s c in next loop, ch 5, d tr c (3 times over hook) in 1st cluster st.

9th Round—Ch 9, s c in next cluster st, * ch 9, s c in next loop, repeat from * twice, ch 9, s c in next cluster st, * ch 9, s c in next loop, repeat from * 12 times, ch 9, s c in next cluster st, * ch 9, s c in next loop, repeat from * twice, repeat from beginning all around ending with ch 5, d tr c in d tr c.

10th Round—* Ch 9, s c in next loop, repeat from * all around, join in d tr c.

11th Round—Ch 1, * 9 s c in next loop, 5 s c, ch 3, 5 s c in next loop, repeat from * all around, join in 1st s c.

12th Round—Sl st to center s c of next loop, * ch 7, shell in next ch 3 loop, ch 7, s c in center s c of next loop, repeat from * all around ending with ch 3, tr c in last sl st.

13th Round—* Ch 3, s c in next loop, ch 9, shell in next shell, ch 9, s c in next loop, repeat from * twice, * ch 3, s c in next loop, ch 7, shell in shell, ch 7, s c in next loop, repeat from * 5 times, * ch 3, s c in next loop, ch 9, shell in next shell, ch 9, s c in next loop, repeat from * once, repeat from beginning all around ending with ch 3, tr tr c (4 times over hook) in tr c.

14th Round—* Ch 11, skip 1 loop, s c in next loop, ch 3, shell in next shell, ch 3, s c in next loop, repeat from * once, ch 9, skip 1 loop, s c in next loop, ch 3, shell in next shell, * ch 3, s c in next loop, ch 7, skip 1 loop, s c in next loop, ch 3, shell in next shell, repeat from * 6 times, ch 3, s c in next loop, ch 9, skip 1 loop, s c in next loop, ch 3, shell in next shell, ch 3, s c in next loop, repeat from beginning all around ending with ch 3, join in tr tr c.

15th Round—Sl st to 4th st of ch, ch 3, cluster st in same space, ch 3, cluster st in same loop, ch 3, cluster st in same loop, ch 3, s c in next loop, * ch 3, shell in next shell, ch 3, s c in next loop, ch 3, 3 cluster sts with ch 3 between each cluster st in next loop, ch 3, s c in next loop, repeat from * once, * ch 3, shell in next shell, ch 3, s c in next loop, ch 3, 2 cluster sts with ch 3 between in next loop, ch 3, s c in next loop, repeat from * 6 times, * ch 3, shell in next shell, ch 3, s c in next loop, ch 3, 3 cluster sts with ch 3 between each cluster st in next loop, ch 3, s c in next loop, repeat from * once, repeat from 1st * all around ending to correspond, join in 1st cluster st.

16th Round—Sl st into loop, ch 4 (counts as part of 1st tr c cluster st), 2 tr c in same space keeping last loop of each tr c on hook, thread over and work off all loops at one time, ch 3, tr c cluster st in next loop (tr c cluster st; 3 tr c in same space keeping last loop of each st on hook, thread over and work off all loops at one time), * ch 8, skip 2 loops, shell in next shell, ch 8, skip 2 loops, tr c cluster st in next loop, ch 3, tr c cluster st in next loop, repeat from * once, ch 8, skip 2 loops, * shell in next shell, ch 6, skip 2 loops, tr c cluster st in next loop, ch 6, skip 2 loops, repeat from * 6 times, shell in next shell, ch 8, skip 2 loops, tr c cluster st in next loop, ch 3, tr c cluster st in next loop, ch 8, shell in next shell, ch 8, skip 2 loops, tr c cluster st in next loop, ch 3, tr c cluster st in next loop, repeat from 1st * all around ending to correspond, join in 1st cluster st.

17th Round—Sl st into loop, ch 4, tr c cluster st in same space, * ch 7, s c in next loop, ch 5, shell in next shell, ch 5, s c in next loop, ch 7, tr c cluster st in next loop, repeat from * once, ch 7, s c in next loop, ch 5, shell in next shell, * ch 4, s c in next loop, ch 9, s c in next loop, ch 4, shell in next shell, repeat from * 6 times, ch 5, s c in next loop, ch 7, tr c cluster st in next loop, ch 7, s c in next loop, ch 5, shell in next shell, ch 5, s c in next loop, ch 7, tr c cluster st in next loop, repeat from 1st * all around ending to correspond, join in 1st cluster st.

18th Round—Sl st into center of next loop, * ch 7, shell in next shell, ch 7, skip 1 loop, s c in next loop, ch 9, s c in next loop, repeat from * once, ch 7, shell in next shell, * ch 7, skip 1 loop, s c in next loop, ch 7, shell in next shell, repeat from * 6 times, ch 7, skip 1 loop, s c in next loop, ch 9, s c in next loop, ch 7, shell in next shell, repeat from * once, ch 7, skip 1 loop, s c in next loop, ch 9, s c in next loop, ch 7, shell in next shell, ch 7, skip 1 loop, s c in next loop, ch 9, s c in next loop, * ch 7, shell in next shell, ch 7, skip 1 loop, s c in next loop, repeat from * 6 times, ch 7, shell in next shell, ch 7, skip 1 loop, s c in next loop, ch 9, s c in next loop, ch 7, shell in next shell, ch 7, skip 1 loop, s c in next loop, ch 9, sl st in last sl st.

19th Round—Sl st to center of next loop, * ch 5, shell in next shell, ch 5, s c in next loop, ch 9, s c in next loop, repeat from * once, ch 5, shell in next shell, * ch 4, s c in next loop, ch 9, s c in next loop, ch 4, shell in next shell, repeat from * 6 times, ch 5, s c in next loop, ch 9, s c in next loop, ch 5, shell in next shell, ch 5, s c in next loop, ch 9, s c in next loop, ch 9, s c in next loop, repeat from 1st * all around ending to correspond, join in last sl st.

20th Round—Sl st to center of shell, ch 4 (counts as part of shell), shell in same space, ** ch 7, skip 1 loop, s c in next loop, ch 7, s c in next loop, ch 7, shell in next shell, ch 9, s c in next loop, ch 7, shell in next shell, * ch 7, skip 1 loop, s c in next loop, ch 7, shell in next shell, repeat from * 6 times, ch 7, skip 1 loop, s c in next loop, ch 9, s c in next loop, ch 7, shell in next shell, ch 7, skip 1 loop, s c in next loop, ch 11, s c in next loop, ch 7, shell in next shell, repeat from ** all around ending to correspond, join in 4th st of ch.

21st Round—Sl st to center of shell, * ch 9, s c in next loop, repeat from * 7 times, * ch 7, s c in next loop, ch 9, s c in next loop, ch 7, s c in next loop, repeat from * 6 times, * ch 9, s c in next loop, repeat from * 7 times, repeat from 1st * all around ending with sl st in sl st.

22nd Round—Start ruffle: s c in next loop, ch 9, s c in same loop, ch 9, s c in same loop, ch 9, s c in same loop, ** ch 9, s c in next loop, * ch 9, s c in same loop, repeat from * twice, repeat from ** all around ending with ch 5, tr tr c in 1st s c.

Next 5 Rounds—* Ch 9, s c in next loop, repeat from * all around ending each round with ch 5, tr tr c in tr tr c.

Next Round—* Ch 5, 2 tr c cluster sts with ch 3 between in next loop, ch 5, s c in next loop, repeat from * all around ending with ch 2, d c in tr tr c.

Next Round—* Ch 5, sl st in 4th st from hook for picot, ch 1, s c in next loop, ch 6, tr c cluster st in next loop, ch 4, sl st in top of cluster st for picot, ch 6, s c in next loop, repeat from * all around, ending with sl st in d c, cut thread. ❀

Mirabella

Materials Required: MERCERIZED CROCHET COTTON, Size 30

4—100 yd. Balls White.
Steel Crochet Hook No. 12.
Doily measures about 7½ inches in diameter without ruffle.
Ch 29, d c in 8th st from hook, * ch 2, skip 2 sts of ch, d c in next st of ch, repeat from * 6 times, ch 13, turn.

2nd Row. D c in 8th st from hook, ch 2, skip 2 sts of ch, d c in next st of ch, ch 2, d c in next d c, (increases at beginning of row) * 2 d c in next mesh, d c in next d c, repeat from * 6 times, 3 d c in end mesh, ch 2, d tr c (3 times over needle) in same space, * ch 2, d tr c over d tr c, repeat from * once (increases at end of row) ch 13, turn.

3rd Row. D c in 8th st from hook, ch 2, skip 2 sts of ch, d c in next st, ch 2, d c in next d tr c, * 2 d c in next mesh, d c in next d tr c, repeat from * once, 2 d c in next mesh, d c in next d c (solid mesh) * ch 2, skip 2 d c, d c in next d c (open mesh) repeat from * 7 times, then work 3 solid meshes, ch 2, d tr c in same space, * ch 2, d tr c over d tr c, repeat from * once, ch 11, turn.

4th Row. D c in 8th st from hook, ch 2, d c in next d tr c, 3 solid meshes, 14 open meshes, 3 solid meshes, increase 2 meshes at end of row. Continue working back and forth according to diagram. To decrease meshes sl st over meshes.

RUFFLE: S c over last d c made, ch 5, s c in next open mesh,

repeat from * around entire doily ending row with ch 1, tr c in 1st s c (this brings thread in position for next row).

2nd Row. 4 s c in same loop, * ch 5, 1 tr c in next loop, ch 2, 2 tr c in same loop, ch 2, 1 tr c in same loop, ch 5, 4 s c in next loop, repeat from * all around ending row with ch 5, 1 tr c in last loop, ch 2, 2 tr c in same loop, ch 2, 1 tr c in same loop, ch 5, sl st in 1st s c.

3rd Row. Ch 4 (counts as 1 tr c) 1 tr c in each of the next 3 s c, ch 5, 1 tr c in next tr c, ch 2, 2 tr c in each of the next 2 tr c, ch 2, 1 tr c in next tr c, ch 5, repeat from beginning all around, join in 4th st of ch.

4th Row. Ch 4, 1 tr c in each of the next 3 tr c, ch 7, 1 tr c in next tr c, ch 2, 1 tr c in each of the next 4 tr e, ch 2, 1 tr c in next tr c, ch 7, repeat from beginning all around in same manner, join in 4th st of ch.

Next 4 Rows. Ch 4, 1 tr c in each of the next 3 tr c, ch 9, 1 tr c in next tr c, ch 2, 1 tr c in each of the next 4 tr c, ch 2, 1 tr c in next tr c, ch 9, repeat from beginning all around in same manner, join in 4th st of ch.

9th Row. Ch 4 (counts as 1 tr c) * thread over needle twice, insert in next tr c, thread over and work off two loops twice, repeat from * twice, thread over and work off all loops at one time, ch 6, sl st in 6th st from hook for picot, * ch 5, sl st in same space, repeat from *, (3 picot cluster) ch 9, tr c in next tr c, ch 5, sl st in top of tr c for picot, ch 3, * thread over needle twice, insert in next tr c, thread over and work off 2 loops twice, repeat from * 3 times, thread over and work off all loops at one time, work a 3 picot cluster, ch 3, tr c in next tr c, ch 5, sl st in top of tr c for picot, ch 9 and continue all around in same manner, join, break thread. ✽

Apple Balm

MATERIALS: J. & P. Coats or Clark's O.N.T. Best Six Cord Mercerized Crochet, *Size 30:* **Small Ball:** J. & P. Coats—7 balls of *White or Ecru,* or 9 balls of *any color,* or Clark's O.N.T.—11 balls of *White or Ecru,* or 15 balls of *any color . . . Steel Crochet Hook No. 10.*

Doily measures 22 inches in diameter

Starting at center, ch 10. Join with sl st to form ring. **1st rnd:** Ch 4, 31 tr in ring. Join. **2nd rnd:** Sc in same place as sl st, * ch 5, skip 1 tr, sc in next tr. Repeat from * around. Join. **3rd rnd:** Sl st to center of next loop, sc in same loop, * ch 13, sc in next loop. Repeat from * around. Join. **4th rnd:** * 7 sc in next loop, (ch 7, sl st in 4th ch from hook—ch 3 and picot made) twice; ch 1, picot, ch 3, picot, ch 3, 7 sc in same loop. Repeat from * around. Join and break off. **5th rnd:** Attach thread to ch-1 sp between picots at top of any loop, ch 12, * dc in next

ch-1 sp of next loop, ch 9. Repeat from * around. Join to 3rd ch of ch-12. **6th rnd:** Ch 6, dc in same place as sl st, * ch 3, skip 4 ch, in next ch make dc, ch 3 and dc; ch 3, in next dc make dc, ch 3 and dc. Repeat from * around. Join. **7th rnd:** Sl st in next sp, ch 4, in same sp make tr, ch 3 and 2 tr; * ch 3, skip next sp, in next sp make 2 tr, ch 3 and 2 tr. Repeat from * around. Join. **8th rnd:** Sl st in next tr and in next sp, ch 3, in same sp make 2 tr, d tr, 2 tr and dc; * ch 3, dc in next sp, ch 3, in next sp make dc, 2 tr, d tr, 2 tr and dc. Repeat from * around. Join. **9th rnd:** Sl st in next 3 sts, ch 14, * d tr in d tr of next scallop, ch 9. Repeat from * around. Join to 5th ch of ch-14. **10th rnd:** 10 sc in each sp around. Join. **11th rnd:** * Ch 3, picot, ch 5, picot, ch 3, skip 4 sc, sc in back loop of next sc. Repeat from * around. Join. **12th rnd:** Sl st to center of loop (between 2 picots), * ch 3, picot, ch 5, picot, ch 3, sc between picots on next loop.

Repeat from * around. Join. **13th to 18th rnds incl:** Repeat 12th rnd. **19th rnd:** Sl st to center of next loop, ch 17, * d tr in next loop between picots, ch 12. Repeat from * around. Join. **20th rnd:** 15 sc in each sp around. Join.

LARGE RUFFLE . . . 1st rnd: * Ch 5, sc in next sc. Repeat from * around. Join. **2nd, 3rd and 4th rnds:** Sl st to center of next loop, sc in same loop, * ch 5, sc in next loop. Repeat from * around. Join. **5th to 9th rnds incl:** Repeat 2nd rnd, making ch-6 loops, instead of ch-5 loops. **10th to 13th rnds incl:** Repeat 2nd rnd, making ch-7 loops. **14th to 17th rnds incl:** Make ch-8 loops around. Join and break off at end of 17th rnd.

SMALL RUFFLE . . . Attach thread to front loop of any sc on 10th rnd and, picking up front loop only, work as for Large Ruffle until 13 rnds are completed. Break off. Starch lightly and press. ❊

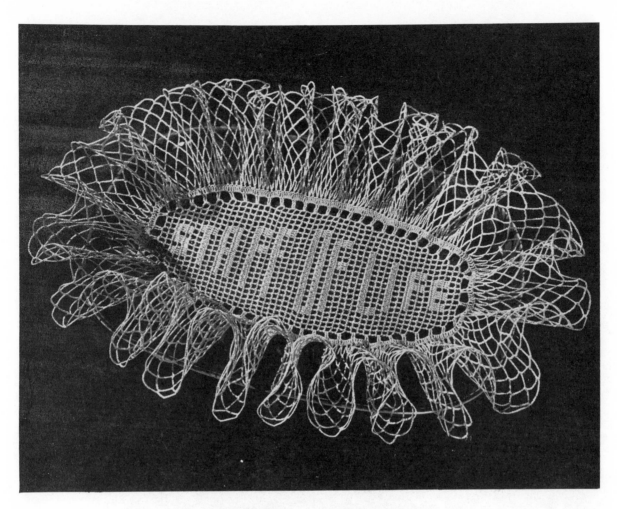

Staff of Life

MATERIALS: J. & P. Coats or Clark's O.N.T. Best Six Cord Mercerized Crochet, *Size 30, 2 balls . . . Steel Crochet Hook No. 10.*

Doily measures 9½ x 13½ inches
NOTE: bl .... **Block**
GAUGE: 5 sps make 1 inch; 5 rows make 1 inch.

Starting at left side of chart, ch 32. **1st row:** Dc in 8th ch from hook (sp made), * ch 2, skip 2 ch, dc in next ch (another sp made). Repeat from * across (9 sps in all). Ch 7, turn. **2nd row:** Dc in next dc (sp increased), * ch 2, skip 2 ch, dc in next dc (sp made over sp). Repeat from * across, ending with ch 2, skip 2 ch of turning chain, dc in next ch, ch 5, dc in same place as last dc (another sp increased). Turn. **3rd row:** Sl st in next 3 ch, ch 5, dc in next dc, 2 more sps, 2 dc in next sp, dc in next dc (bl made), 1 sp, 3 bls, 3 sps. Ch 7, turn. **4th row:** Inc 1 sp, make 3 more sps, dc in next 3 dc (bl made over bl), ch 2, skip 2 dc, dc in next dc (sp made

over bl), 1 bl, 1 sp, 1 bl, 3 sps, inc 1 sp. Turn. **5th row:** Sl st in next 3 ch, ch 5 and follow chart across. Continue following chart until 34 rows are completed. **35th row:** Sl st in next 2 ch and in next dc (1 sp decreased), ch 5, and follow chart across to within last sp (another sp decreased). Ch 5, turn. Now follow chart to end. Do not break off at end of last row, but work in rnds along outer edges as follows: **1st rnd:** Ch 4, turn, tr in same place, ch 4, 2 tr in same place, ch 4, skip 2 sps, 2 tr in next sp, ch 4, skip 1 sp, 2 tr in next

sp, ch 4, in corner st of end-sp make 2 tr, ch 4 and 2 tr; ch 4, 2 tr in next sp, * ch 4, skip 1 sp, 2 tr in next sp. Repeat from * around, working over other end of doily to correspond. Join to 4th st of ch-4 first made. **2nd rnd:** Ch 3 (to count as dc), dc in each ch and each tr around. Join. Hereafter do not join rnds. **3rd rnd:** * Ch 11, skip 1 dc, sc in next dc. Repeat from * around. **4th to 12th rnds incl:** * Ch 11, sc in next loop. Repeat from * around. Break off at end of 12th rnd. Starch lightly and press. ✽

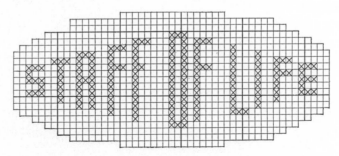

Rugged Ruffled Doily

Materials Required: AMERICAN THREAD COMPANY "DE LUXE" MERCERIZED CROCHET AND KNITTING COTTON, ARTICLE 346

1—300 yd. Ball White and 1—200 yd. Ball Yellow or any contrasting Color.
Steel Crochet Hook No. 7.
Doily measures 7½ inches in diameter without the ruffle.
With Yellow, ch 6, join to form a ring, ch 1 and work 8 s c in ring, join.

2nd Row. * Ch 8, s c in next s c, repeat from * all around ending row with ch 3, tr c in 1st s c (this brings thread in position for next row) .

3rd Row. Ch 5, s c in same loop, * ch 5, s c in next loop, ch 5, s c in same loop (picot loop), repeat from * all around, ch 5, join in same space as 1st ch.

4th Row. Sl st into picot loop, ch 3, 2 d c in same space, ch 3, 3 d c in same space, * ch 5, skip 1 loop, 3 d c, ch 3, 3 d c (shell) in next picot loop, repeat from * all around, ch 5, join in 3rd st of ch, break Yellow.

5th Row. Attach White in center of shell, ch 3, 2 d c, ch 3, 3 d c in same space, * ch 5, shell in center of next shell, repeat from * all around, ch 5, join in 3rd st of ch.

6th Row. Sl st to center of shell, shell in same space, * ch 5, s c over the White and Yellow loop of 2 previous rows, ch 5, shell in center of next shell, repeat from * all around ending row with ch 5, s c over loops of two previous rows, ch 5, join.

7th Row. Sl st to center of shell, shell in same space, * ch 4, s c in next loop, ch 5, s c in next loop, ch 4, shell in center of next shell, repeat from * all around ending row with ch 4, s c in next loop, ch 5, s c in next loop, ch 4, join in 3rd st of ch.

8th Row. Sl st to center of shell, shell in same space, * ch 5, skip 1 loop, 1 tr c, ch 3, 1 tr c in next loop, ch 5, skip 1 loop, shell in center of next shell, repeat from * all around in same manner ending row to correspond, join.

9th Row. Sl st to center of shell, shell in same space, * ch 5, skip 1 loop, shell in ch 3 loop, ch 5, skip 1 loop, shell in center of next shell, repeat from * all around in same manner ending row to correspond, join.

10th Row. Sl st to center of shell, shell in same space, * ch 5, s c over next loops of previous 2 rows, ch 5, shell in center of next shell, repeat from * all around in same manner ending row to correspond, join.

11th Row. Same as 7th row.

12th Row. Sl st to center of shell, shell in same space, * ch 5, skip 1 loop, s c in next loop, ch 5, skip 1 loop, shell in center of next shell, repeat from * all around in same manner ending row to correspond, join.

13th Row. Sl st to center of shell, shell in same space, ** ch 5, * thread over needle twice, insert in next loop, pull through and work off 2 loops twice, repeat from *, thread over and work off remaining loops at one time, ch 5, shell in center of next shell, repeat from ** all around in same manner ending row to correspond, join.

14th Row. Sl st to center of shell, * ch 8, skip the 5 ch loop, 2 d c in next st, ch 8, skip the 5 ch loop, s c in center of next shell, repeat from * all around in same manner ending row to correspond, break White.

15th Row. Attach Yellow in next loop, ch 3, 2 d c, ch 3, 3 d c (shell) in same loop, * ch 3, 3 d c, ch 3, 3 d c in next loop, repeat from * all around, ch 3, join in 3rd st of ch.

16th Row. Sl st to center of shell, ch 4, d c in same space, * ch 1, d c in same space, repeat from * 3 times, * ch 2, 6 d c with ch 1 between each d c in next loop, ch 2, 6 d c with ch 1 between each d c in center of next shell, repeat from * all around ending row to correspond, ch 2, join.

17th Row. Ch 4, * d c in next ch 1 loop, ch 1, d c in next ch 1 loop, ch 1, d c in next d c, ch 1, d c in next ch 1 loop, ch 1, d c in next d c, ch 1, d c in next ch 1 loop, ch 1, d c in next ch 1 loop, ch 1, d c in next d c, ch 2, skip the ch 2 loop, d c in next d c, ch 1, repeat from * all around in same manner ending row to correspond, ch 2, join in 3rd st of ch (9 d c in each section with ch 1 between each d c) .

18th Row. Ch 4, ** d c in next loop, * ch 1, d c in next loop, repeat from * twice, ch 1, d c in next d c, * ch 1, d c in next loop, repeat from * 3 times, ch 1, d c in next d c, ch 2, skip the ch 2 loop, d c in next d c, ch 1, repeat from ** all around in same manner ending row to correspond, ch 2, join (11 d c in each d c section with ch 1 between each d c) .

19th Row. Ch 4, ** d c in next loop, * ch 1, d c in next loop, repeat from * 8 times, ch 1, d c in next d c, ch 2, skip the ch 2 loop, d c in next d c, ch 1, repeat from ** all around in same manner ending row to correspond, ch 2, join (12 d c in each section with ch 1 between each d c) , break Yellow.

EDGE: Attach White in same space (1st d c of d c section) s c in same space, * ch 3, sl st in 3rd st from hook for picot, s c in next loop, s c in next d c, repeat from * 23 times, drop loop from hook, insert needle in 11th picot made, pick up loop and pull loop through (this scallop lays in front of work) , s c in next ch 1 loop of next d c section, s c in next d c, * ch 3, sl st in 3rd st from hook for picot, s c in next loop, s c in next d c, repeat from * 10 times, drop loop from hook, insert needle in 12th picot of 2nd scallop, pick up loop and pull through having 1 picot between joinings (this scallop lays to back of work) , ** s c in 1st ch 1 loop of next d c section, s c in next d c, * picot, s c in next loop, s c in next d c, repeat from * 10 times, drop loop from hook, insert needle in 10th free picot of previous scallop, pick up loop and pull through leaving 1 picot free between joinings (this scallop lays to front of work) , repeat from ** all around having 1 scallop to back of work and the next to front of work to the last scallop. On last scallop work 9 picots after the joining, then join to 13th picot made at beginning of row, s c in next loop, s c in next d c, picot, s c in next loop, s c in next d c, join to 10th free picot of previous scallop, break thread. ✿

Spiked Spiral

Shown in color on the inside back cover.

Materials Required:
AMERICAN THREAD COMPANY
The Famous "PURITAN" STAR SPANGLED
 MERCERIZED CROCHET COTTON, Article 40
3 balls Silver Spangle
2 balls Cinnamon Spangle or colors of your choice
App. size: 22 inches in diameter
Steel Crochet Hook No. 5
With Silver Spangle chain (ch) 6, join to form a ring, ch 4, work 23 treble crochet (trc) in ring, join in 4th stitch (st) of ch. 2nd ROUND: Ch 5, skip 1 trc, sc in next trc, repeat from beginning 10 times, ch 2, skip 1 trc, double crochet (dc) in joining st (this brings thread in position for next round). 3rd ROUND: Ch 5, sc in next loop, repeat from beginning all around ending with ch 2, dc in dc. 4th and 5th ROUNDS: Ch 6, sc in next loop, repeat from beginning all around ending with ch 3, dc in dc. 6th ROUND: Ch 8, sc in next loop, repeat from beginning all around ending with ch 4, trc in dc. 7th ROUND: Ch 8, sc in next loop, repeat from

beginning all around ending with ch 8, join in trc. 8th ROUND: Slip stitch (sl st) into 1st st of ch, ch 3, 1 dc in each st of ch all around, join in ch 3. 9th ROUND: Ch 6, skip 3 dc, sc in next dc, repeat from beginning all around ending with ch 3, dc in joining. 10th ROUND: Same as 4th round. 11th and 12th ROUNDS: Ch 7, sc in next loop, repeat from beginning all around ending with ch 3, dc in dc. 13th and 14th ROUNDS: Same as 6th and 7th rounds. 15th ROUND: Same as 8th round. 16th ROUND: Same as 9th round. 17th ROUND: Same as 4th round. 18th and 19th ROUNDS: Same as 12th round. 20th and 21st ROUNDS: Same as 6th and 7th rounds, cut Silver Spangle. 22nd ROUND: Attach Cinnamon Spangle in joining and repeat 8th round, cut Cinnamon Spangle. 23rd ROUND: Attach Silver Spangle in last dc, ch 6, dc in same dc, ch 6, skip the ch 3 and 1 dc, sc in next dc, * ch 6, skip 2 dc, 2 dc with ch 3 between in next dc, ch 6, skip 2 dc, sc in next dc, repeat from * all around ending to correspond, join. 24th ROUND: Sl st to
continued on page 36

Periwinkle

Materials Required:
AMERICAN THREAD COMPANY
The Famous "PURITAN" MERCERIZED
   CROCHET COTTON, Article 40
2 balls White or
The Famous "PURITAN" STAR SPANGLED
   MERCERIZED CROCHET COTTON, Article 40
3 balls Silver Spangle or color of your choice
Steel Crochet Hook No. 7
App. size: 16 inches in diameter for "PURITAN";
  18 inches in diameter for "PURITAN" STAR
  SPANGLED

Chain (ch) 5, slip stitch (sl st) in 5th st from hook for picot, ch 4, keeping last loop of each double crochet (dc) on hook work 6 dc in 1st st of ch, thread over and work off all loops at one time, repeat from beginning 3 times, join in 1st picot. 2nd ROUND: Ch 20, single crochet (sc) in same space, repeat from beginning twice, ch 4, dc in 1st st of ch, ch 5, sl st in 1st st of ch for picot, ch 4, dc in 1st st of ch, sc in next picot, repeat from beginning all around. 3rd ROUND: Sl st across 8 sts of ch, * ch 4, keeping last loop of each dc on hook work 6 dc in same loop, thread over and work off all loops at one time (a cluster st), ch 5, sl st in

top of cluster st for picot, ch 4, sc in same loop, ch 4, dc in 1st st of ch, sc in next loop, repeat from * twice, but ending 2nd repeat with sc in next picot, ch 4, dc in 1st st of ch, sc in next loop, then repeat from 1st * all around ending to correspond, join. 4th ROUND: Sl st to picot, ch 4, 8 treble crochet (trc) in same picot, * ch 4, sc in next picot, ch 5, sc in same picot, ch 4, 9 trc in next picot, repeat from * all around ending to correspond, join in 4th st of ch. 5th ROUND: Ch 3, 2 dc in same space, * ch 2, skip 1 trc, 3 dc in next trc, repeat from * 3 times, ch 2, sc in next loop, 7 dc in next loop (scallop), sc in next loop, ch 2, 3 dc in 1st trc, repeat from 1st * all around ending to correspond, join in 3rd st of ch. 6th ROUND: Sl st in 1st ch 2 loop, ch 3, 2 dc in same space, * ch 3, 3 dc in next loop, repeat from * twice, ch 7, sc in center dc of scallop, ch 5, sc in same space, ch 7, skip the next ch 2 loop, 3 dc in next ch 2 loop and repeat from 1st * all around ending to correspond, join in 3rd st of ch. 7th ROUND: Sl st to ch 3 loop, ch 3, 2 dc in same space, * ch 4, 3 dc in next loop, repeat from * once, ch 5, sc in next loop, 9 dc scallop in next loop, sc in next loop, ch 5, 3 dc in next loop and repeat from 1st * all around ending to correspond, join in
continued overleaf

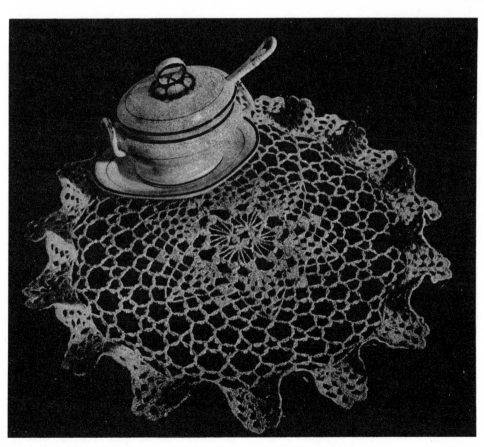

PERIWINKLE (continued)

3rd st of ch. 8th ROUND: Sl st to loop, ch 3, 2 dc in same space, * ch 4, 3 dc in next loop, ch 6, sc in next loop, ch 6, sc in center dc of scallop, ch 5, sc in same space, ch 6, sc in next loop, ch 6, 3 dc in next loop, repeat from * all around ending to correspond, join in 3rd st of ch. 9th ROUND: Sl st to loop, ch 3, 2 dc in same space, * ch 5, 3 dc in same space, ch 5, sc in next loop, ch 4, dc in 1st st of ch (rice st), ch 5, sl st in 1st st of ch for picot, rice st, sc in next loop, 9 dc scallop in next loop, sc in next loop, rice st, picot, rice st, sc in next loop, ch 5, 3 dc in next loop, repeat from * all around ending to correspond, join in 3rd st of ch. 10th ROUND: Sl st to loop, ch 3, 2 dc in same space, * ch 5, sc in next loop, rice st, picot, rice st, sc in next picot, rice st, picot, rice st, sc in center dc of scallop, rice st, picot, rice st, sc in next picot, rice st, picot, rice st, sc in next loop, ch 5, 3 dc in next loop, repeat from * all around ending to correspond, join in 3rd st of ch. 11th ROUND: Sl st to next dc, * rice st, picot, rice st, sc in next picot, repeat from * 3 times, rice st, picot, rice st, sc in center dc of dc group, repeat from 1st * all around ending to correspond, join. 12th ROUND: Sl st to picot, * rice st, picot, repeat from * once, rice st, sc in next picot, repeat from 1st * all around, join. 13th ROUND: Sl st to picot, * rice st, picot, rice st, sc in next picot, rice st, sc in next picot, repeat from * all around, join. 14th and 15th ROUNDS: Repeat 12th and 13th rounds. 16th ROUND: Sl st to picot, ch 6, 8 trc with ch 2 between each trc in same space, * ch 4, 9 trc with ch 2 between each trc in next picot, repeat from * all around ending with ch 4, join in 4th st of ch. 17th ROUND: Sl st to loop, ch 3, 2 dc in same space, ** ch 3, skip 1 loop, 3 dc in next loop, ch 3, 3 dc in center trc, * ch 3, skip 1 loop, 3 dc in next loop, repeat from * once, sc in next loop, 3 dc in next loop, repeat from ** all around ending to correspond, join. 18th ROUND: Sl st to loop, ch 3, 2 dc in same space, ** ch 3, 3 dc in next loop, ch 3, 3 dc in center dc of next dc group, * ch 3, 3 dc in next loop, repeat from * once, 3 dc in next loop, repeat from ** all around ending to correspond, join. 19th ROUND: Sl st to loop, ch 3, 2 dc in same space, ** ch 4, 3 dc in next loop, ch 4, 3 dc in center dc of dc group, * ch 4, 3 dc in next loop, repeat from * once, sc between next 2 groups of 3 dc, 3 dc in next loop, repeat from ** all around ending to correspond, join. 20th ROUND: Sl st to loop, * 3 sc in loop, sc in next dc, ch 4, skip 1 dc, sc in next dc, 6 dc in next loop, skip 1 dc, sc in next dc, 6 dc in next loop, sc in next dc, ch 4, skip 1 dc, sc in next dc, 3 sc in next loop, sc in next dc, ch 2, skip 2 dc, 1 sc and 2 dc, sc in next dc, repeat from * all around, join, cut thread. ✴

SPIKED SPIRAL (continued from page 34)

loop, ch 6, dc in same loop, * ch 5, sc in next loop, repeat from * once, ch 5, 2 dc with ch 3 between in next loop, repeat from 1st * all around, join. 25th ROUND: Sl st to loop, ch 6, dc in same loop, * ch 5, sc in next loop, repeat from * twice, ch 5, 2 dc with ch 3 between in next loop, repeat from 1st * all around, join. 26th ROUND: Sl st to loop, ch 6, dc in same loop, * ch 5, sc in next loop, repeat from * 3 times, ch 5, 2 dc with ch 3 between in next loop, repeat from 1st * all around, join. 27th ROUND: Sl st to loop, ch 6, dc in same loop, * ch 5, sc in next loop, repeat from * 4 times, ch 5, 2 dc with ch 3 between in next loop, repeat from 1st * all around, join, cut Silver Spangle. 28th ROUND: Join Cinnamon Spangle in 1st loop, ch 6, dc in same loop, * ch 5, sc in next loop, repeat from * 5 times, ch 5, 2 dc with ch 3 between in next loop, repeat from 1st * all around, join. 29th ROUND: Sl st to loop, ch 6, dc in same loop, * ch 5, sc in next loop, repeat from * 6 times, ch 5, 2 dc with ch 3 between in next loop, repeat from 1st * all around, join, cut thread. Starch and pin as illustrated. ✴

SHOOTING STAR (continued from page 23)

18th Row. Ch 8, s c in center st of next shell, ch 8, s c in next loop, repeat from beginning all around ending row with ch 1, d tr c in tr c.

19th Row. Start ruffle, * ch 10, s c in same loop, repeat from * twice, ch 10, s c in next loop, repeat from beginning all around ending row with ch 5, tr tr c (4 times over needle) in d tr c (224 loops).

20th and 21st Rows. Ch 10, s c in next loop, repeat from beginning all around ending row with ch 5, tr tr c in tr tr c.

22nd Row. * Ch 9, s c in next loop, repeat from * 4 times, ch 9, 2 shells with ch 5 between in center st of next loop, ch 9, s c in next loop, repeat from beginning all around in same manner ending row with ch 5, tr tr c in tr tr c.

23rd Row. * Ch 9, s c in next loop, repeat from * 5 times, ch 2, shell in center st of next shell, ch 3, s c in next 5 ch loop, ch 3, shell in center st of next shell, ch 2, s c in next loop, repeat from beginning all around ending row with sl st.

24th Row. Sl st to center of loop, * ch 9, s c in next loop, repeat from * 4 times, ch 3, shell in center st of next shell, ch 3, s c in next loop, ch 3, s c in next loop, ch 3, shell in center st of next shell, ch 3, s c in next ch 9 loop, repeat from * all around in same manner, join.

25th Row. Sl st to center of loop, * ch 9, s c in next loop, ch 2, 2 shells with ch 3 between in center st of next loop, ch 2, s c in next loop, ch 9, s c in next loop, ch 3, shell in center st of next shell, ch 3, s c in next loop, ch 7, s c in next loop, ch 7, s c in next loop, ch 3, shell in center st of next shell, ch 3, s c in next ch 9 loop, repeat from * all around in same manner, join.

26th Row. Sl st to center of loop, * ch 3, shell in center st of next shell, ch 3, s c in next loop, ch 5, sl st in s c for picot, ch 3, shell in center st of next shell, ch 3, s c in next loop, ch 4, 3 d c, 5 ch picot, 2 d c in center st of next shell, ch 3, s c in next loop, ch 3, s c in next loop, ch 9, sl st in 5th st from hook for picot, ch 4, s c in next loop, ch 3, s c in next loop, ch 3, 3 d c, 5 ch picot, 2 d c in center st of next shell, ch 4, s c in next loop, repeat from * all around in same manner, join, break thread. ✴

Frilly Tiger Lily

MATERIALS—Lily Pearl Cotton, size 5:—8-balls Ivory, and 3-balls Orange (or other colors). Crochet hook size 5.

In Ivory, ch 2, 8 sc in 1st st. In back lps, sl st in 1st sc, ch 3, 2 dc in same st, (ch 1, 3 dc in next sc) 7 times, ch 1, sl st in 1st 3-ch. Work following rows in both lps. **ROW 2**—Ch 5, turn, (1 dc in next dc, 2 dc in next, 1 dc in next, ch 2) repeated around. Sl st in 3d st of 5-ch. **ROW 3**—Ch 3, turn, * (2 dc in next dc) twice, 1 dc in next, ch 2, 1 dc in next dc. Repeat from * around and join to 1st 3-ch. **ROW 4**—Ch 5, turn, (1 dc in next dc, 2 dc in next, 1 dc in next, ch 1, 1 dc in next dc, 2 dc in next, 1 dc in next, ch 2) repeated around. Sl st in 3d st of 5-ch. **ROW 5**—Ch 3, turn, 1 dc in each dc with 2-ch between all dc-groups. **ROW 6**—Ch 6, turn, 1 dc in each dc with 3-ch between groups. Join to 3d st of 6-ch. **ROW 7**—Like Row 5 with 4-chs between groups. **ROW 8**—Ch 9, turn, (4 dc, ch 4, 4 dc, ch 6) repeated around. Sl st in 3d st of 9-ch. **ROW 9**—Ch 3, turn, 3 dc. Make 4-chs over 4-chs, and 8-chs over 6-chs. **ROW 10**—Ch 13, turn, 4 dc. Make 4-chs over 4-chs, and 10-chs over 8-chs. **ROW 11**—Ch 3, turn, 3 dc. Make 13-chs over 10-chs. **ROW 12**—Ch 9, turn, (3 dc in center st of 13-ch, ch 6, dc in 4 dc, ch 4, 4 dc, ch 6) repeated around. Sl st in 3d st of 1st 9-ch. **ROW 13**—Ch 3, turn, 3 dc, * ch 4, 4 dc, ch 6, 2 dc in next dc, 1 dc in next, 2 dc in next, ch 6, 4 dc. Repeat from * around and join. **ROW 14**—Ch 9, turn, * 2 dc in next dc, (1 dc in next, 2 dc in next) twice, ch 6, 4 dc, ch 3, 4 dc, ch 6. Repeat from * around and join to 3d st of 9-ch. **ROW 15**—Ch 3, turn, 3 dc, * ch 2, 4 dc, ch 8, 8 dc, ch 8, 4 dc. Repeat from * around and join. **ROW 16**—Ch 13, turn, (8 dc, ch 10, 4 dc, ch 1, 4 dc, ch 10) repeated around. Sl st in 3d st of 13-ch. **ROW 7**—Ch 3, turn, * dc in next 2 sts made into one st (a decrease), dc in next 2 dc, a dec. in next 2 sts, dc in next, ch 5, 2 dc in 5th st of 10-ch, ch 6, 8 dc, ch 6, 2 dc in 6th st of 10-ch, ch 5, 1 dc in next dc. Repeat from * around and join. **ROW 18**—Ch 9, turn, * (2 dc in next dc) twice, ch 7, (a dec. in next 2 dc, 1 dc in next) twice, a dec. in next 2 dc, ch 7, (2 dc in next dc) twice, ch 6, 1 dc in next dc, 2 decs. 1 dc in end dc, ch 6. Repeat from * around and join to 3d st of 9-ch. **ROW 19**—Ch 3, turn, * a dec., 1 dc in next st, ch 7, 4 dc, ch 9, a dec. in next 2 dc, 1 dc in next st, a dec. in next 2 dc, ch 9, 4 dc, ch 7, 1 dc. Repeat from * around and join. **ROW 20**—Ch 11, turn, * 4 dc, ch 11, (dc in next 3 dc) worked off into one st, ch 11, 4 dc, ch 8, (dc in 3 dc) made into one st, ch 8. Repeat from * around and join to 3d st of 11-ch. **ROW 21**—Ch 14, turn, * (a dec. in next 2 dc) twice, ch 12, 1 dc in next dc-Cluster, ch 12, 2 dec. in next group, ch 9, tr in next dc-Cluster, ch 9. Repeat from * around and join to 5th st of 14-ch. **ROW 22**—Ch 12, turn, a dec. in next 2 dc, ch 13, 1 dc in next dc, ch 13, a dec. in next 2 dc, ch 10, 1 dc in next tr, ch 10. Repeat from * around and join to 3d st of 13-ch. **ROW 23**—Ch 14, turn, * dc in next dc, (ch 14, dc in next dc) twice, ch 11, dc in next dc, ch 11. Repeat from * around and join to 3d st of 14-ch. Repeat once. **ROW 25**—Ch 5, dc in next 3d st, (ch 2, dc in next 3d st) repeated around and join to 3d st of 5-ch. **ROW 26**—Ch 3, turn, (2 dc in 2-ch, 1 dc in dc) repeated around and join. **ROW 27**—Turn, (ch 5, sc in next 4th dc) 108 times. **ROW 28**—Ch 1, turn, sl st in next lp, ch 3, 2 dc in same lp, (ch 3, 3 dc in next lp) repeated around and join. **ROW 29**—Ch 1, turn, sl st in sp, ch 3, (1 dc, ch 2 and 2 dc) in same sp, * ch 3, (2 dc, ch 2 and 2 dc) in next sp. Repeat from * around and

join. **ROW 30**—Ch 1, turn, sl st in 3-ch sp, ch 5, (a 2-dc, ch 2 and 2-dc shell in 2-ch sp of next shell, ch 2, 1 dc in next sp, ch 2) repeated around and join to 3d st of 5-ch. **ROW 31**—Ch 4, turn, * dc in next sp, ch 1, a shell in next shell, ch 1, dc in next sp, ch 1, dc in next dc, ch 1. Repeat from * around and join to 3d st of 4-ch. **ROW 32**—Ch 1, turn, sl st in next 1-ch sp, ch 5, dc in next sp, * ch 2, a shell in next shell, (ch 2, dc in next sp) 4 times. Repeat from * around and join to 3d st of 5-ch. Fasten off. **ROW 33**—Turn and join Orange to one shell, ch 3, (dc, ch 2, 2 dc) in same place, * (ch 2, dc in next sp) 5 times, ch 2, a shell in next shell. Repeat from * around and join. Fasten off. **ROW 34**—With Ivory, repeat last row to *. * (Ch 2, dc in next sp) 6 times, ch 2, a shell in next shell. Repeat from * around and join. Fasten off. **EDGE**—Turn and join color to 2d dc to left of one shell, (ch 1, 2 sc in next sp) 5 times, ch 2, 2 sc in shell, ch 3, sl st in last sc for a p, 1 sc in shell, ch 2, 2 sc in next sp, (ch 1, 2 sc in next sp) 4 times, ch 1, drop lp from hook, insert hook in 1st 1-ch, catch lp and pull thru (a border loop), * 2 sc in next sp, ch 1, 2 sc in next, ch 2, (2 sc, a p and 1 sc) in shell, ch 2, 2 sc in next sp, (ch 1, 2 sc in next sp) 4 times, ch 1, drop lp from hook, insert hook in 2d 1-ch sp to left of shell in last border loop (this 1-ch sp is directly over 2d dc to left of shell). Draw dropped lp thru. Repeat from * around. **Fasten off.**

Stretch and pin center of doily right-side-down on a true circle. Steam and press center dry thru a cloth. Moisten back and inside of border loops by patting and rubbing with a cloth pad dipped in thin, hot starch. Remove and pin center right-side-up on same circle. Stretch border loops and pin down back row. Shape border loops evenly with fingers. Let remain until dry. ✤

Summer Breeze

Materials Required:
MERCERIZED CROCHET COTTON, size 30
1 ball White without ruffle
3 balls White with ruffle
Steel crochet hook No. 12
Approximate size: 12½ inches in diameter without ruffle

or

The Famous "PURITAN" MERCERIZED CROCHET COTTON, Article 40 or
"DE LUXE" Quality MERCERIZED CROCHET COTTON, Article 346
2 balls White without ruffle
5 balls White with ruffle
Steel crochet hook No. 7
Approximate size: 17½ inches in diameter without ruffle.

Chain (ch) 6, join to form a ring, ch 1 and work 8 single crochet (s c) in ring, join in 1st s c.

2nd Round. Ch 3, 2 double crochet (d c) in same space keeping last loop of each d c on hook, thread over and work off all loops at one time, * ch 4, cluster stitch (st) in next s c (cluster st: 3 d c in same space keeping last loop of each d c on hook, thread over and work off all loops at one time), repeat from * 6 times, ch 4, join in top of 1st cluster st.

3rd Round. Ch 1, s c in same space, * 5 s c in next loop, s c in next cluster st, repeat from * all around ending with 5 s c in last loop, join.

4th Round. Ch 8, skip 2 s c, treble crochet (tr c) in next s c, * ch 4, skip 2 s c, tr c in next s c, repeat from * all around, ch 4, join in 4th st of ch.

5th Round. S c in same space, ch 4, sl st in same space for picot, * 5 s c over next loop, s c in next tr c, ch 4, sl st in top of last s c for picot, repeat from * all around ending with 5 s c over last loop, join.

6th Round. Slip stitch (sl st) to 3rd s c, ch 4, 2 tr c in same space, * ch 5, 3 tr c in center s c of next scallop, repeat from * all around, ch 5, join.

7th Round. Ch 1, s c in same space, 1 s c in each of the next 2 tr c, * 5 s c over next loop, 1 s c in each of the next 3 tr c, repeat from * all around ending with 5 s c over next loop, join.

8th Round. Sl st to next s c, ch 6, * skip 3 s c, 1 d c, ch 2, 1 d c in next s c, ch 3, skip 3 s c, d c in next s c, ch 3, repeat from * all around ending to correspond, join in 3rd st of ch.

9th Round. Ch 6, * skip 1 loop, 5 tr c in next loop, ch 2, skip 1 loop, tr c in next d c, ch 2, repeat from * all around ending to correspond, join in 4th st of ch.

10th Round. * Ch 4, 1 tr c in each of the next 5 tr c, ch 4, s c in next tr c, repeat from * all around, join.

11th Round. Sl st to 1st tr c, ch 4, 1 tr c in each of the next 4 tr c keeping last loop of each tr c on hook, thread over and work off all loops at one time, * ch 7, 1 tr c in each of the next 2 loops keeping last loop of each tr c on hook, thread over and work off all loops at one time, ch 7, 1 tr c in each of the next 5 tr c keeping last loop of each tr c on hook, thread over and work off all loops at one time, repeat from * all around ending to correspond, ch 7, join in top of 1st cluster.

12th Round. Ch 1, s c in same space, * ch 4, sl st in top of s c just made for picot, 7 s c over next loop, s c in joined tr c, ch 4, sl st in top of s c just made for picot, 7 s c over next loop, s c in next cluster, repeat from * all around ending to correspond, join.

13th Round. Sl st to 4th s c, then work same as 6th round.

14th Round. 1 s c in each tr c and 7 s c over each loop, join.

15th Round. Sl st to next s c, ch 6, * skip 4 s c, 1 d c, ch 2, 1 d c in next s c, ch 3, skip 4 s c, d c in next s c, ch 3, repeat from * all around ending to correspond, join.

Repeat the 9th, 10th and 11th Rounds.

19th Round. Same as 12th round but working 5 s c over each loop instead of 7 s c.

20th and 21st Rounds. Same as 6th and 7th rounds.

22nd Round. Sl st to next s c, ch 7, skip 3 s c, tr c in next s c, * ch 3, skip 3 s c, tr c in next s c, repeat from * all around, ch 3, join in 4th st of ch.

23rd Round. Ch 4, * 3 tr c in next loop, tr c in next tr c, 3 tr c in next loop, tr c in next tr c, ch 3, tr c in next tr c, ch 3, tr c in next tr c, repeat from * all around ending to correspond, ch 3, join in 4th st of ch.

24th Round. Sl st to next tr c, ch 4, 1 tr c in each of the next 6 tr c, * ch 4, skip 1 loop, 1 tr c in next tr c, ch 4, skip 1st tr c of next tr c group, 1 tr c in each of the next 7 tr c, repeat from * all around ending to correspond, ch 4, join.

25th Round. Sl st to next tr c, ch 4, 1 tr c in each of the next 4 tr c, * ch 4, skip 1 loop, 1 tr c, ch 3, 1 tr c in next tr c, ch 4, skip 1st tr c of next tr c group, 1 tr c in each of the next 5 tr c, repeat from * all around ending to correspond, ch 4, join.

26th Round. Sl st to next tr c, ch 4, 1 tr c in each of the next 2 tr c keeping last loop of each tr c on hook, thread over and work off all loops at one time, * ch 7, skip 1 loop, 1 tr c, ch 3, 1 tr c in next loop, ch 7, skip 1st tr c of next tr c group, work a tr c cluster over next 3 tr c, repeat from * all around ending to correspond, ch 7, join.

27th Round. * Ch 4, s c in same space, ch 6, skip 1 loop, 7 tr c in next loop, ch 6, s c in top of next cluster, repeat from * all around, join.

28th Round. Sl st to 1st tr c of next tr c group, ch 5, tr c in next tr c, * ch 1, tr c in next tr c, repeat from * 4 times, * ch 4, 1 tr c in each of the next 2-ch 6 loops keeping last loop of each tr c on hook, thread over and work off all loops at one time, ch 4, 1 tr c in each of the next 7 tr c with ch 1 between each tr c, repeat from * all around ending to correspond, ch 4, join.

29th Round. Ch 3, counts as part of 1st cluster st, d c in same space, ch 3, sl st in top of st just made for picot, * ch 3, skip 1 tr c, 2 d c cluster st in next tr c (2 d c cluster st: 2 d c in same space keeping last loop of each d c on hook, thread over and work off all loops at one time), ch 3, sl st in top of cluster st for picot, repeat from * twice, ch 3, skip 4 sts of ch, 2 d c cluster st in next st where the 2 tr c are joined together, ch 3, sl st in top of cluster st for picot, ch 3, 2 d c cluster st in next tr c, ch 3 picot, repeat from 1st * all around ending to correspond, ch 3, join, cut thread if ruffle is not desired.

30th Round. Start ruffle: Sl st to next loop, ch 8, tr c in next loop, * ch 4, tr c in next loop, repeat from * all around ending with ch 4, join in 4th st of ch.

31st Round. * Ch 6, s c in next loop, ch 6, s c in next tr c, ch 6, s c in next loop, ch 6, s c in same loop, ch 6, s c in next tr c, repeat from * all around ending with ch 3, d c in same space as beginning.

32nd Round. * Ch 6, s c in next loop, repeat from * all around ending with ch 3, d c in d c. Repeat the last round 10 times ending last round with ch 6, s c in d c.

Next Round. Sl st into loop, ch 4, 6 tr c in same loop, ** ch 3, s c in next loop, * ch 6, s c in next loop, repeat from * twice, ch 3, 7 tr c in next loop, repeat from ** all around ending to correspond, ch 3, join in 4th st of ch.

Next Round. Ch 5, 1 tr c in each of the next 6 tr c with ch 1 between each tr c, * ch 4, skip 1 loop, s c in next loop, ch 6, s c in next loop, ch 6, s c in next loop, ch 4, 1 tr c in each of the next 7 tr c with ch 1 between each tr c, repeat from * all around ending to correspond, ch 4, join in 4th st of ch.

Next Round. Ch 3, d c in same space, ** ch 3, sl st in top of last st for picot, * ch 3, s c in next tr c, ch 3, 2 d c cluster st in next tr c, ch 3, sl st in top of cluster st for picot, repeat from * twice, * ch 3, s c in next s c, ch 3, 2 d c cluster st in next loop, ch 3 picot, repeat from * once, ch 3, s c in next s c, ch 3, 2 d c cluster st in next tr c, repeat from ** all around ending to correspond, ch 3, join, cut thread. ✽

Snowflake Swirl

Make this doily with any of the
AMERICAN THREAD COMPANY products listed below:

Material	Quantity	Approx. Size of Doily without Ruffle	Size of Needle
"GEM" CROCHET COTTON Article 35, size 30	2 balls White	8 inches in diameter	steel 11 or 12
or			
"PURITAN" CROCHET COTTON Article 40	2 balls White	11½ inches in diameter	steel 7
or			
"DE LUXE" CROCHET COTTON Article 346	2 balls White	11½ inches in diameter	steel 7

Ch 6, join to form a ring, ch 1 and work 12 s c in ring, join in 1st s c.

2nd Round—Ch 7, tr c in next s c, * ch 3, tr c in next s c, repeat from * 9 times, ch 3, join in 4th st of ch.

3rd Round—Ch 1, * 2 s c, ch 3, 2 s c in next loop, repeat from * all around, join in 1st s c.

4th Round—Sl st to center of next loop, ch 7, 3 tr c in same loop, * ch 5, s c in next ch 3 loop, ch 5, 3 tr c, ch 3, 3 tr c in next ch 3 loop, repeat from * 4 times, ch 5, s c in next ch 3 loop, ch 5, 2 tr c in next ch 3 loop already worked in, join in 4th st of ch.

5th Round—Ch 1, ** 1 s c, ch 3, 1 s c in next loop, ch 7, * tr c in next loop keeping last loop of st on hook, repeat from * once, thread over and work off the 3 loops at one time (tr c cluster), ch 7, repeat from ** all around, join in 1st s c.

6th Round—Sl st to center of loop, ch 7, 4 tr c in same space, * ch 5, skip 1 loop, 1 s c, ch 3, 1 s c in top of tr c cluster, skip 1 loop, ch 5, 4 tr c, ch 3, 4 tr c in next loop, repeat from * 4 times, ch 5, 1 s c, ch 3, 1 s c in top of tr c cluster, ch 5, 3 tr c in 1st loop already worked in, join in 4th st of ch.

7th Round—Ch 1, * 1 s c, ch 3, 1 s c in next loop, ch 7, s c in next loop, ch 9, s c in next large loop, ch 7, repeat from * all around, ending with ch 3, tr c in 1st s c (this brings thread in position for next round).

8th Round—Ch 7, tr c in top of tr c just made, * ch 7, 1 tr c, ch 3, 1 tr c in center st of next large loop, repeat from * all around, ending with ch 7, join in 4th st of ch.

9th Round—Ch 1, * 3 s c in next loop, 3 s c, ch 3, 3 s c in next loop, repeat from * all around, join in 1st s c.

10th Round—Sl st to next s c, * ch 5, 1 tr c, ch 3, 1 tr c in next ch 3 loop, ch 5, s c in center s c of next 3 s c group, repeat from * all around ending with ch 2, d c in sl st.

11th Round—Ch 4, tr c in next loop, ** ch 3, 3 tr c, ch 3, 3 tr c in next loop, ch 3, * tr c in next loop keeping last loop of st on hook, repeat from * once, thread over and work off all 3 loops at one time, repeat from ** all around ending with ch 3, join in 4th st of ch.

12th Round—Ch 1, s c in same space, ch 3, s c in next tr c, skip 1 loop, ch 7, 1 s c, ch 3, 1 s c in next loop, * ch 7, 1 s c, ch 3, 1 s c in next tr c cluster, ch 7, skip 1 loop, 1 s c, ch 3, 1 s c in next loop, repeat from * all around ending with ch 3, tr c in 1st s c.

13th Round—* Ch 9, s c in next large loop, repeat from * all around ending with ch 4, d tr c (3 times over hook) in tr c.

14th Round—Same as last round ending with ch 4, d tr c in d tr c.

15th Round—Ch 7, tr c in top of d tr c just made, * ch 7, 1 tr c, ch 3, 1 tr c in center st of next loop, repeat from * all around ending with ch 7, join in 4th st of ch.

16th Round—Same as 9th round.

17th Round—Sl st to next s c, * ch 4, 1 tr c, ch 3, 1 tr c in next ch 3 loop, ch 4, s c in center s c of next 3 s c group, repeat from * all around ending with ch 1, d c in sl st.

18th Round—Ch 4, tr c in next loop, ** ch 2, 3 tr c, ch 3, 3 tr c in next loop keeping last loop of st on hook, repeat from * once, thread over and work off all loops at one time, repeat from ** all around ending with ch 2, join in 4th st of ch.

19th Round—Ch 3, s c in same space, ch 5, 1 s c, ch 3, 1 s c in next ch 3 loop, ch 5, 1 s c, ch 3, 1 s c in next tr c cluster, ch 5, 1 s c, ch 3, 1 s c in next ch 3 loop, repeat from * all around ending with ch 2, d c in joining.

20th Round—* Ch 9, s c in next large loop, repeat from * all around ending with ch 4, d tr c in d c.

21st Round—* Ch 9, s c in next loop, repeat from * all around ending with ch 4, d tr c.

22nd Round—2 tr c in same d tr c of previous round, ch 3, 2 tr c in same space, s c in next loop, * ch 9, s c in next loop, 2 tr c, ch 3, 2 tr c in next s c, s c in next loop, repeat from * all around ending with ch 4, d tr c in d tr c.

23rd Round—* Ch 9, 1 s c, ch 3, 1 s c in next ch 3 loop, ch 9, s c in next loop, repeat from * all around ending with ch 4, d tr c in d tr c.

24th Round—* Ch 9, s c in next ch 9 loop, repeat from * all around ending with ch 4, d tr c in d tr c.

25th Round—* Ch 7, s c in next loop, repeat from * all around ending with ch 7, sl st in d tr c.

26th Round—**Start ruffle:** sl st into loop, s c in same loop, * ch 10, s c in same loop, repeat from * once, * ch 10, s c in next loop, ch 10, s c in same loop, ch 10, s c in same loop, repeat from * all around ending with ch 5, tr tr c (4 times over hook) in 1st s c.

27th Round—* Ch 9, s c in next loop, repeat from * all around ending with ch 4, d tr c in tr tr c.

28th Round—Same as last round ending with ch 4, d tr c in d tr c.

29th Round—Same as 22nd round.

30th Round—Same as 23rd round.

31st and 32nd Rounds—Same as 24th round.

33rd Round—* Ch 9, s c in next loop, 2 tr c, ch 3, 2 tr c in next s c, s c in next loop, repeat from * all around ending to correspond.

34th Round—Sl st to 3rd st of next loop, 1 s c, ch 3, 1 s c in same loop, * ch 7, sl st in 4th st from hook for picot, ch 3, 1 s c, ch 3, 1 s c in next loop, repeat from * all around, cut thread. ✿

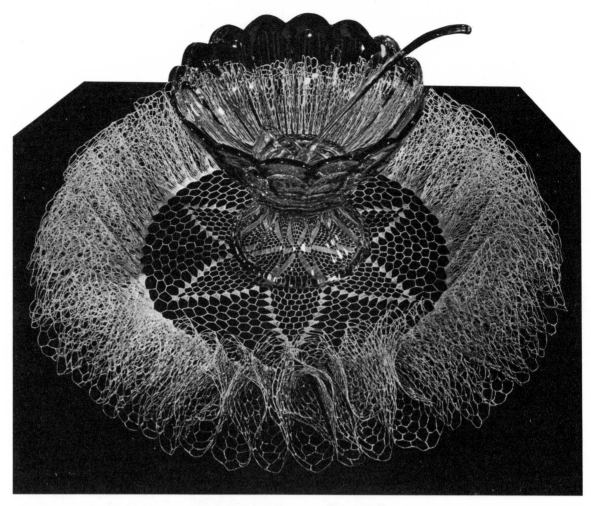

North Star

MATERIALS: J. & P. Coats or Clark's O.N.T. Best Six Cord Mercerized Crochet, *Size 30:* **Small Ball:** J. & P. Coats—*7 balls of White or Ecru, or 9 balls of any color, or* Clark's O.N.T.—*11 balls of White or Ecru, or 15 balls of any color . . . Steel Crochet Hook No. 10.*

Centerpiece measures 28 inches in diameter

Starting at center, ch 9. Join with sl st to form ring. **1st rnd:** Ch 9, (tr in ring, ch 5) 5 times. Join to 4th ch of ch-9. **2nd rnd:** Sl st in next sp, ch 4, 6 tr in same sp, * ch 5, 7 tr in next sp. Repeat from * around, ending with ch 5. Join. **3rd rnd:** Ch 4, tr in next 6 tr, * ch 5, tr in next sp, ch 5, tr in next 7 tr. Repeat from * around. Join. **4th rnd:** Ch 4, tr in next 6 tr, * (ch 5, tr in next sp) twice; ch 5, tr in next 7 tr. Repeat from * around. Join. **5th to 10th rnds incl:** Work as for 4th rnd, having 1 sp more between tr groups on each rnd. **11th rnd:** Ch 9, * skip next tr group, 7 tr in next sp, (ch 5, tr in next sp) 7 times; ch 5, 7 tr in next sp, ch 5. Repeat from * around, ending with 6 tr in last sp, sl st in 4th ch of ch-9. **12th rnd:** Sl st in next 3 ch, ch 9, * 7 tr in next sp, (ch 5, tr in next sp) 6 times; ch 5, 7 tr in next sp, ch 5, tr in next sp, ch 5. Repeat from * around, ending with ch 2, dc in 4th ch of ch-9. **13th rnd:** Ch 9, tr in next sp, * ch 5, 7 tr in next sp, (ch 5, tr in next sp) 5 times; ch 5, 7 tr in next sp, (ch 5, tr in next sp) twice. Repeat from * around. Join as for last rnd. **14th rnd:** Ch 10, (tr in next sp, ch 6) twice; * 7 tr in next sp, (ch 5, tr in next sp) 4 times; ch 5, 7 tr in next sp, (ch 6, tr in next sp) 3 times; ch 6. Repeat from * around, ending with ch 3, dc in 4th ch of ch-10. **15th rnd:** Ch 11, (tr in next sp, ch 7) 3 times; * 7 tr in next sp, (ch 5, tr in next sp) 3 times; ch 5, 7 tr in next sp, (ch 7, tr in next sp) 4 times; ch 7. Repeat from * around, ending with ch 3, tr in 4th ch of ch-11. **16th rnd:** Ch 12, (tr in next sp, ch 8) 4 times; * 7 tr in next sp, (ch 5, tr in next sp) twice; ch 5, 7 tr in next sp, (ch 8, tr in next sp) 5 times; ch 8. Repeat from * around, ending with ch 4, tr in 4th ch of ch-12. **17th rnd:** Ch 12, (tr in next sp, ch 8) 5 times; * 7 tr in next sp; ch 5, tr in next sp, ch 5, 7 tr in next sp, (ch 8, tr in next sp) 6 times; ch 8. Repeat from * around, joining as last rnd. **18th rnd:** Ch 13, (tr in next sp, ch 9) 6 times; * 7 tr in next sp, ch 5, 7 tr in next sp, (ch 9, tr in next sp) 7 times; ch 9. Repeat from * around, ending with ch 4, d tr in 4th ch of ch-13. **19th rnd:** Ch 13, (tr in next sp, ch 9) 7 times; * 7 tr in next sp, (ch 9, tr in next sp) 8 times; ch 9. Repeat from * around, joining as last rnd. **20th rnd:** Ch 14, (tr in next sp, ch 10) 8 times; * skip 3 tr of next tr group, tr in next tr, (ch 10, tr in next sp) 9 times; ch 10. Repeat from * around. Join as before. **21st rnd:** Ch 15, * tr in next sp, ch 11. Repeat from * around. Join with sl st to 4th ch of ch-15. **22nd rnd:** 15 sc in each sp around. Join.

RUFFLE . . . 1st rnd: * Ch 7, sc in next sc. Repeat from * around. Join. **2nd and 3rd rnds:** Sl st to center of next loop, ch 9, * tr in next loop, ch 5. Repeat from * around. Join with sl st to 4th ch of ch-9. **4th, 5th and 6th rnds:** Sl st to center of next sp, ch 11, * tr in next sp, ch 7. Repeat from * around. Join. **7th, 8th and 9th rnds:** Sl st to center of next sp, ch 13, * tr in next sp, ch 9. Repeat from * around. Join. **10th, 11th and 12th rnds:** Sl st to center of next sp, ch 15, * tr in next sp, ch 11. Repeat from * around. Join and break off. Starch lightly and press. ❋

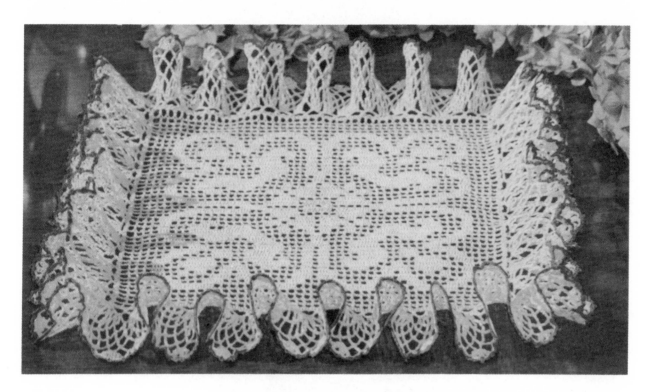

St. Elmo's Fire

Materials Required: AMERICAN THREAD COMPANY
"GEM" CROCHET COTTON, Article 35, size 30
1 ball each White and Medium Blue or
"STAR" CROCHET COTTON, Article 20, size 30
2 balls White and 1 ball Medium Blue
Doily measures 7½ inches square without the ruffle.
Steel crochet hook No. 12.

With White ch 146, d c in 8th st from hook, * ch 2, skip 2 sts of ch, d c in next st of ch, repeat from * across ch (47 meshes), ch 5, turn.

2nd Row—D c in next d c, * ch 2, d c in next d c (open mesh), repeat from * across row ending with ch 2, d c in 3rd st of end ch, ch 5, turn. Repeat the last row twice.

5th Row—D c in next d c, * ch 2, d c in next d c, repeat from * 4 times, * 2 d c in next mesh, d c in next d c (solid mesh), repeat from * 4 times, 5 open meshes, 5 solid meshes, 5 open meshes, 5 solid meshes, 5 open meshes, 5 solid meshes, 6 open meshes, ch 5, turn. Continue working back and forth according to chart working 4 rows of open meshes at top same as at lower edge, do not turn at end of last row.

EDGE: Working on side work 2 s c in same mesh, * s c in next mesh, ch 2, s c in same mesh, repeat from * to corner mesh, in corner mesh work 2 s c, ch 4, 2 s c, repeat from 1st * all around ending with 2 s c in 1st corner mesh, ch 1, d c in 1st s c (this brings thread in position for next row).

2nd Row—Ch 6, s c over the d c just made, ** ch 6, s c in same space, ch 6, s c in same space, ch 6, s c in next ch 2 loop, * ch 6, skip next ch 2 loop, s c in next ch 2 loop, repeat from * 21 times, ch 6, s c in corner loop, ch 6, s c in same space, repeat from ** all around in same manner, join.

3rd Row—Sl st into 1st loop at corner, ch 7, s c in same space, ch 7, s c in same space, * ch 7, s c in next loop, ch 7, s c in same space, ch 7, s c in same space, repeat from * all around ending with ch 3, tr c in sl st.

4th Row—* Ch 7, s c in next loop, repeat from * all around ending with ch 3, tr c in tr c. Repeat the last row 3 times.

Shown in color on the back cover.

8th Row—* Ch 4, 2 tr c in center st of next loop keeping last loop of each tr c on hook, thread over and work off all loops at one time (a 2 tr c cluster st), ch 3, 2 tr c cluster st in same space, ch 3, 2 tr c cluster st in same space, ch 4, s c in next loop, repeat from * all around, cut White.

Next Row—Attach Blue in top of 1st cluster st, * ch 3, s c in same space, ch 3, s c in top of next cluster st, ch 3, s c in same space, ch 3, s c in top of next cluster st, ch 3, s c in same space, ch 4, sl st in next s c, ch 4, s c in top of next cluster st, repeat from * all around ending to correspond, join, cut thread. ✻

Clarissa

Shown in color on the inside back cover.

Materials Required: AMERICAN THREAD COMPANY
"PURITAN" CROCHET COTTON, Article 40 or
"DE LUXE" CROCHET COTTON, Article 346
2 balls White
1 ball Kelly Green or any contrasting color
Steel crochet hook No. 7.
Doily measures about 8¼ inches in diameter without ruffle.
With White ch 6, join to form a ring, ch 1 and work 8 s c with ch 3 between each s c in ring, ch 3, join in 1st s c.

2nd Round—Sl st to loop, ch 3 (counts as part of 1st cluster st), 2 d c in same space keeping last loop of each st on hook, thread over and work off all loops at one time, * ch 5, cluster st in next loop (cluster st: 3 d c in loop keeping last loop of each st on hook, thread over and work off all loops at one time), repeat from * 6 times, ch 2, d c in top of 1st cluster st (this brings thread in position for next round).

3rd Round—Ch 3, s c in same loop, * ch 7, 1 s c, ch 3, 1 s c in next loop, repeat from * 6 times, ch 3, d c in same loop.

4th Round—Ch 3, 2 d c in d c just made, * ch 5, 3 d c, ch 3, 3 d c in center st of next loop, repeat from * 6 times, ch 5, 3 d c in same space with 1st group of d c, ch 3, join in 3rd st of ch.

5th Round—Ch 3, 1 d c in each of the next 2 d c keeping last loop of each st on hook, thread over and work off all loops at one time, * ch 5, s c in next loop, ch 5, 1 d c in each of the next 3 d c keeping last loop of each st on hook, thread over and work off all loops at one time, repeat from * all around ending with ch 5, s c in last loop, ch 2, d c in top of 1st cluster st.

6th Round—Ch 5, s c in next loop, repeat from beginning all around ending with ch 2, d c in d c.

7th Round—Ch 6, s c in next loop, repeat from beginning all around ending with ch 3, d c in d c.

8th Round—Ch 7, s c in next loop, repeat from beginning all around working last s c in d c.

9th Round—Sl st to center of next loop, ch 3, 2 d c in same space, ch 3, 3 d c in same space, * ch 5, s c in next loop, ch 3, 3 d c, ch 3, 3 d c in center st of next loop, repeat from * all around ending with ch 3, s c in next loop, ch 3, join in 3rd st of ch.

10th Round—Ch 3, 1 d c in each of the next 2 d c keeping last loop of each st on hook, thread over and work off all loops at one time, * ch 5, s c in next loop, ch 5, 1 d c in each of the next 3 d c keeping last loop of each d c on hook, thread over and work off all loops at one time, ch 5, skip 2 loops, 1 d c in each of the next 3 d c keeping last loop of each d c on hook, thread over and work off all loops at one time, repeat from * 14 times, ch 5, s c in next loop, ch 5, 1 d c in each of the next 3 d c keeping last loop of each d c on hook, thread over and work off all loops at one time, ch 2, d c in 1st cluster st.

11th Round—Ch 7, s c in next loop, repeat from beginning all around ending with ch 3, tr c in d c.

12th and 13th Rounds—Same as last round but ending each round with ch 3, tr c in tr c.

14th Round—Ch 3, 2 d c in tr c just worked keeping last loop of each st on hook, thread over and work off all loops at one time, * ch 6, cluster st in center st of next loop, repeat from * all around ending with ch 3, tr c in cluster st.

15th Round—Ch 9, d c in next loop, * ch 6, d c in next loop, repeat from * all around ending with ch 6, join in 3rd st of ch.

16th Round—Sl st into next loop, ch 3, 2 d c, ch 3, 3 d c in same loop, * ch 1, 3 d c, ch 3, 3 d c (shell) in next loop, repeat from * all around, ch 1, join in 3rd st of ch.

17th Round—Sl st to center of shell, ch 4, d c in same space, * ch 1, d c in same space, repeat from * 5 times, * ch 2, 8 d c with ch 1 between each d c in center of next shell, repeat from * all around, ch 2, join.

18th Round—Ch 4, ** d c in next ch 1 loop, * ch 1, d c in next ch 1 loop, ch 1, d c in next d c, repeat from * 3 times, ch 1, d c in next ch 1 loop, ch 1, d c in next d c, ch 2, skip 1 d c, d c in next d c, ch 1, repeat from ** all around in same manner ending to correspond, ch 2, join in 3rd st of ch (13 d c in each section with ch 1 between each d c).

19th Round—Ch 4, ** d c in next loop, * ch 1, d c in next loop, repeat from * 4 times, ch 1, d c in next d c, * ch 1, d c in next loop, repeat from * 5 times, ch 1, d c in next d c, ch 2, skip the ch 2 loop, d c in next d c, ch 1, repeat from ** all around in same manner ending to correspond, ch 2, join (15 d c in each d c section).

20th Round—Ch 4, ** d c in next loop, * ch 1, d c in next loop, repeat from * 12 times, ch 1, d c in next d c, ch 2, skip the ch 2 loop, d c in next d c, ch 1, repeat from ** all around in same manner ending to correspond, ch 2, join (16 d c in each section), cut thread.

EDGE: Attach Green in next d c, s c in same space, * ch 3, sl st in 3rd st from hook for picot, s c in next loop, s c in next d c, repeat from * 30 times, s c in next loop, ch 1, drop loop from hook, insert hook in 14th picot made, pick up loop and pull loop through (this scallop lays in front of work), s c in next d c, * s c in next loop, s c in next d c, ch 3, sl st in 3rd st from hook for picot, repeat from * 14 times, s c in next loop, s c in next d c, ch 1, drop loop from hook, insert hook in 16th free picot of 2nd scallop, pick up loop and pull through having 1 picot between joinings (this scallop lays to back of work), ch 1, ** s c in next loop, s c in next d c, * picot, s c in next loop, s c in next d c, repeat from * 14 times, ch 1, drop loop from hook, insert hook in 14th free picot of previous scallop, pick up loop and pull through leaving 1 picot free between joinings, ch 1 (this scallop lays to front of work), repeat from ** all around having 1 scallop to back of work and the next to front of work to the last scallop, on last scallop work 13 picots after the joining, s c in next loop, s c in next d c, then ch 1, join to 16th picot made at beginning of round, ch 1, s c in next loop, s c in next d c, picot, s c in next loop, ch 1, join to 14th free picot of scallop before last, ch 1, join, cut thread. ❄

Octopus Ruffled Doily

Shown in color on the inside front cover.

Materials Required: AMERICAN THREAD COMPANY
"PURITAN" CROCHET COTTON, Article 40 or
"DE LUXE" CROCHET COTTON, Article 346

1 ball each White and Kelly Green or any contrasting color
Steel crochet hook No. 7.
Doily measures about 17 inches in diameter.

With White ch 5, join to form a ring, ch 1 and work 10 s c in ring, join in 1st s c.

2nd Round—Ch 5, d c in next s c, * ch 2, d c in next s c, repeat from * all around, ch 2, join in 3rd st of ch.

3rd Round—Ch 1, s c in same space, * 2 s c in next loop, s c in next d c, repeat from * all around ending with 2 s c in next loop, join.

4th Round—Ch 3, 2 d c in same space, * ch 3, skip 2 s c, 3 d c in next s c, repeat from * all around, ch 3, join in 3rd st of ch.

5th Round—Ch 3, 1 d c in each of the next 2 d c, * 3 d c over next loop, 1 d c in each of the next 3 d c, repeat from * all around ending with 3 d c over next loop, join in 3rd st of ch.

6th Round—Ch 3, d c in same space, ch 2, 2 d c in same space, * ch 3, skip 2 d c, d c in next d c, ch 3, skip 2 d c, 2 d c, ch 2, 2 d c (shell) in next d c, repeat from * all around ending with ch 3, skip 2 d c, d c in next d c, ch 3, join.

7th Round—Sl st to center of shell, ch 3, 1 d c, ch 2, 2 d c in same space, * ch 3, skip 1 loop, d c in next d c, ch 3, shell in next shell, repeat from * all around ending to correspond, ch 3, join.

8th Round—Sl st to center of shell, ch 3, 1 d c, ch 2, 2 d c in same space, * ch 3, skip 1 loop, 3 d c in next d c, ch 3, shell in next shell, repeat from * all around ending to correspond, ch 3, join.

9th Round—Sl st to center of shell, ch 3, 1 d c, ch 2, 2 d c in same space, * ch 3, skip 1 loop, 2 d c in next d c, d c in next d c, 2 d c in next d c, ch 3, shell in next shell, repeat from * all around ending to correspond, ch 3, join.

10th Round—Work in same manner as last round increasing 1 d c at beginning and end of each d c group.

11th Round—Sl st into shell, ch 3, 1 d c, ch 2, 2 d c in same space, * ch 3, skip 1 loop, s d c in next d c (s d c, thread over hook, insert in st, pull loop through, thread over and work off all loops at one time), 1 d c in next d c, 2 d c in next d c, 3 tr c in next d c, 2 d c in next d c, 1 d c in next d c, s d c in next d c, ch 3, shell in next shell, repeat from * all around ending to correspond, ch 3, join.

12th Round—Sl st to center of shell, * ch 3, sl st in same space, ch 10, sl st in center st of next scallop, ch 3, sl st in same space, ch 10, sl st in center of next shell, repeat from * all around ending with ch 5, d tr c (3 times over hook) in 1st sl st.

13th Round—Ch 3, sl st in same space, * ch 10, sl st in next ch 10 loop, ch 3, sl st in same space, repeat from * all around ending with ch 10, join in d tr c.

14th Round—Sl st into next loop, ch 3, 8 d c in same space, * ch 9, sl st in next loop, ch 3, sl st in same space, ch 9, 9 d c over next loop, repeat from * all around ending with ch 9, sl st in next loop, ch 3, sl st in same space, ch 9, join.

15th Round—Sl st to next d c, ch 3, 1 d c in each of the next 6 d c, * ch 9, sl st in center st of next loop, ch 3, sl st in same space (picot), ch 11, picot in center st of next loop, ch 9, skip 1 d c , 1 d c in each of the next 7 d c, repeat from * all around ending to correspond, ch 9, join.

16th Round—Sl st to next d c, ch 3, 1 d c in each of the next 4 d c, * ch 9, picot in center st of next loop, ch 9, sl st in center st of next loop, ch 10, sl st in same space, ch 21, sl st in same space, ch 10, sl st in same space, ch 9, picot in center st of next loop, ch 9, skip 1 d c, 1 d c in each of the next 5 d c, repeat from * all around ending to correspond, ch 9, join.

17th Round—Sl st to next d c, ch 3, 1 d c in each of the next 2 d c, * ch 9, picot in center st of next loop, ch 9, s c in next loop, ch 9, s c in next loop, ch 9, sl st in center st of next long loop, ch 10, sl st in same space, ch 21, sl st in same space, ch 10, sl st in same space, ch 9, s c in next loop, ch 9, s c in next loop, ch 9, picot in center st of next loop, ch 9, skip 1 d c, 1 d c in each of the next 3 d c, repeat from * all around ending to correspond, ch 9, join.

18th Round—Sl st to next d c, ch 6, sl st in 3rd st from hook for picot, ** ch 9, picot in center st of next loop, * ch 9, s c in next loop, repeat from * 3 times, ch 9, sl st in center st of next long loop, ch 10, sl st in same space, ch 21, sl st in same space, ch 10, sl st in same space, * ch 9, s c in next loop, repeat from * 3 times, ch 9, picot in center st of next loop, ch 9, skip 1 d c, d c in next d c, ch 3, sl st in top of d c for picot, repeat from ** all around in same manner ending with ch 4, d tr c in 3rd st of ch.

19th Round—* Ch 9, s c in next loop, repeat from * 6 times, ** ch 9, sl st in center st of next long loop, ch 10, sl st in same space, ch 21, sl st in same space, ch 10, sl st in same space, * ch 9, s c in next loop, repeat from * 13 times, repeat from ** all around ending to correspond, joining last ch 9 in d tr c, cut White.

20th Round—Attach Green in center st of next loop, ch 3, sl st in same space, * ch 9, picot in center st of next loop, repeat from * 6 times, ** ch 9, picot in next ch 10 loop, ch 9, picot in center st of next long loop, ch 9, picot in center of next ch 10 loop, * ch 9, picot in center st of next loop, repeat from * 14 times, repeat from ** all around ending to correspond, join, cut Green. ✻

Flying Comet

MATERIALS: J. & P. Coats or Clark's O.N.T. Best Six Cord Mercerized Crochet, *Size 30:* **Small Ball:** J. & P. Coats—3 balls of *White or Ecru,* or Clark's O.N.T.—4 balls of *White or Ecru* . . . Steel Crochet Hook No. 10.

Doily measures 13 inches in diameter

Starting at center, ch 9. Join with sl st to form ring. **1st rnd:** 16 sc in ring, sl st in first sc made. **2nd rnd:** Sc in same place as sl st, * ch 5, skip 1 sc, sc in next sc. Repeat from * around, ending with ch 5, sl st in first sc. **3rd rnd:** Sc in same place as sl st, * 2 sc in ch-5 sp, ch 4, sc in next sc. Repeat from * around, ending with sl st in first sc. **4th to 15th rnds incl:** * Sc in next sc and in each remaining sc of sc group, 2 sc in ch-4 sp, ch 4, skip first sc of next sc-group. Repeat from * around (15 sc in each sc group on last rnd). Join as before. **16th rnd:** * Sc in next 13 sc, ch 4, sc in ch-4 sp, ch 4, skip next sc. Repeat from * around. Join. **17th rnd:** * Sc in next 11 sc, (ch 5, sc in next loop) twice; ch 5, skip next sc. Repeat from * around. Join. Continue in this manner, having 2 sc less in each sc group and 1 loop more between sc groups on each rnd, until 1 sc remains in each sc group, ending with ch 2, dc in first sc. Now work as follows: **1st rnd:** * Ch 2, sc in next loop, (ch 5, sc in next loop) 7 times. Repeat from * around, ending with ch 2, dc in dc. **2nd rnd:** * Ch 5, skip ch-2 loop, sc in next loop, (ch 5, sc in next loop) 6 times. Repeat from * around, ending as previous rnd. **3rd and 4th rnds:** * Ch 5, sc in next loop. Repeat from * around, ending with ch 2, dc in dc. **5th rnd:** Ch 5, sc in next loop, * ch 5, 6 dc in next loop; (ch 5, sc in next loop) 6 times. Repeat from * around. Join as before. **6th rnd:** (Ch 5, sc in next loop) twice; * ch 5, sc between 3rd and 4th dc of dc group, (ch 5, sc in next loop) 7 times. Repeat from * around. Join. **7th rnd:** * Ch 5, sc in the next loop. Repeat from * around. Join. **8th rnd:** * Ch 5, sc in next loop. Repeat from * around, ending with ch-5, sl st in dc. **9th rnd:** 6 sc in each loop around.

RUFFLE . . . 1st rnd: * Ch 5, skip 1 sc, sc in next sc. Repeat from * around. Join. **2nd to 5th rnds incl:** Sl st to center of next loop, sc in same loop, * ch 5, sc in next loop. Repeat from * around. Join. **6th to 10th rnds incl:** Sl st to center of next loop, sc in same loop, * ch 6, sc in next loop. Repeat from * around. Join. **11th to 18th rnds incl:** Repeat 2nd rnd, making ch-7 loops on the 11th to 15th rnds incl, ch-8 loops on 16th rnd, ch-9 loops on 17th rnd and ch-10 loops on 18th rnd. Join and break off. Starch lightly and press. ✻

DOVER BOOKS ON QUILTING, CROCHET, KNITTING AND OTHER AREAS

The United States Patchwork Pattern Book, Barbara Bannister and Edna P. Ford. (23243-3) $2.75

State Capitals Quilt Blocks, Barbara Bannister and Edna Paris Ford (eds.). (23557-2) $2.95

Mittens to Knit, Mary Lamb Becker. (24577-2) $2.95

Small Patchwork Projects, Barbara Brondolo. (24030-4) $3.95

Knitted Toys and Dolls, Nellie Burnham. (24148-3) $1.95

Easy-to-Make Appliqué Quilts for Chilren, Judith Corwin. (24293-5) $3.50

Design and Make Your Own Floral Appliqué, Eva Costabel-Deutsch. (23427-4) $2.95

Knit Your Own Norwegian Sweaters, Dale Yarn Company. (23031-7) $3.75

Easy-to-Make Felt Ornaments, Betty Deems. (23389-8) $3.50

Smocking, Dianne Durand. (23788-5) $2.00

Easy and Attractive Gifts You Can Sew, Jane Ethe and Josephine Kirshon. (23638-2) $3.95

Early American Patchwork Patterns, Carol Belanger Grafton. (23882-2) $3.50

Quilting Manual, Dolores A. Hinson. (23924-1) $3.50

Nova Scotia Patchwork Patterns, Carter Houck. (24145-9) $3.50

Big Book of Stuffed Toy and Doll Making, Margaret Hutchings, (24266-8) $6.95

Teddy Bears and How to Make Them, Margaret Hutchings. (23487-8) $6.95

The Standard Book of Quilt Making and Collecting, Marguerite Ickis. (20582-7) $4.95

Crocheted Cats and Kittens, Barbara and Ruth Jacksier. (24527-6) $2.50

Filet Crochet, Mrs. F. W. Kettelle. (23745-1) $2.25

First Book of Modern Lace Knitting, Marianne Kinzel. (22904-1) $3.95

Second Book of Modern Lace Knitting, Marianne Kinzel. (22905-X) $4.25

Paperbound unless otherwise indicated. Prices subject to change without notice. Available at your book dealer or write for free catalogues to Dept. Needlework, Dover Publications, Inc., 31 East 2nd Street, Mineola, N.Y. 11501. Please indicate field of interest. Each year Dover publishes over 200 books on fine art, music, crafts and needlework, antiques, languages, literature, children's books, chess, cookery, nature, anthropology, science, mathematics, and other areas.

Manufactured in the U.S.A.